Walden

BY HAIKU

Ian Marshall

Walden

BY HAIKU

The University of Georgia Press

Athens and London

© 2009 by the University of Georgia Press

Athens, Georgia 30602

www.ugapress.org

All rights reserved

Designed by Mindy Basinger Hill

Set in 9.5/15 Electra LT Standard

Printed and bound by Thomson-Shore

The paper in this book meets the guidelines for
permanence and durability of the Committee on
Production Guidelines for Book Longevity of the
Council on Library Resources.

Printed in the United States of America

13 12 11 10 09 C 5 4 3 2 1

Library of Congress Cataloging-in-Publication Data

Marshall, Ian, 1954–

Walden by haiku / Ian Marshall.

    p.   cm.

Includes bibliographical references and index.

ISBN-13: 978-0-8203-3288-8 (alk. paper)

ISBN-10: 0-8203-3288-7 (alk. paper)

1. Thoreau, Henry David, 1817–1862. Walden — Poetry.

2. Thoreau, Henry David, 1817–1862 — Criticism and
interpretation. 3. Haiku, American.

4. Natural history — Massachusetts — Walden Woods —
Poetry. 5. Walden Woods (Mass.) — Poetry. I. Title.

PS3613.A77347 W35 2009

811'.6 — dc22   2008048367

British Library Cataloging-in-Publication Data available

FOR MEGAN,

The Hiker Formerly Known as Mooseless

"Shall we always study to obtain more of these things, and not sometimes to be content with less?"

—Henry David Thoreau, "Economy"

Contents

Acknowledgments   xi

Introduction: To Be Content with Less   xiii

PART ONE. *Walden* by Haiku
   Economy   3
   Where I Lived, and What I Lived For   8
   Reading   12
   Sounds   17
   Solitude   23
   Visitors   28
   The Bean-Field   31
   The Village   36
   The Ponds   42
   Baker Farm   48
   Higher Laws   51
   Brute Neighbors   54
   House-Warming   57
   Former Inhabitants; and Winter Visitors   61
   Winter Animals   66
   The Pond in Winter   70
   Spring   77
   Conclusion   84

PART TWO. Sources and Commentary
   Introduction   99
   Economy   102
   Where I Lived, and What I Lived For   107
   Reading   111
   Sounds   114
   Solitude   124
   Visitors   130

The Bean-Field   134

The Village   142

The Ponds   146

Baker Farm   157

Higher Laws   162

Brute Neighbors   167

House-Warming   172

Former Inhabitants; and Winter Visitors   179

Winter Animals   187

The Pond in Winter   195

Spring   202

Conclusion   213

Notes   227

Works Cited   231

Index   235

Acknowledgments

I am grateful to the friends, scholars, and colleagues who read parts or all of this manuscript at various stages of its development and generously shared their suggestions, ideas, expertise, encouragement, and enthusiasm about haiku, Thoreau, and/or nature writing. Specifically, I'd like to thank David Barnhill, Mike Branch, John Elder, Richard Hunt, Rochelle Johnson, Dinty W. Moore, Sandy Petrulionis, Megan Simpson, Laura Dassow Walls, Michael Dylan Welch, and Ken Womack. Thanks as well to my fellow members of the Association for the Study of Literature and Environment for ongoing inspiration and camaraderie. I'm happy to be part of the tribe.

Introduction

To Be Content with Less

The Poet stands by a pond, looking, listening. He lingers long and long, sees the seasons change, thinks of our lives in nature, finds contact, connection. He hears the sound of water and visualizes the jump of a frog, sees the surface of the pond dimple and imagines the busy lives of fish. Swallows skim the surface, a loon cackles. The pond freezes over, melts, ice drifts to the shore, conifers lean over the pond. The Poet watches, he listens. And he wonders about the depth of the pond, wonders what it all means. Are these phenomena of life representative of some deeper spiritual truth? Or are they meaningful in and of themselves, making and displaying their own deeper meaning? He notes the ongoing changes of the natural world, sees that they all add up to constancy, finds the eternal in the ephemeral.

Returning to his hut, he writes it all down, what he saw and what he thinks, and the ephemeral stuff of language, too, is somehow rendered into something eternal. For years and years, for generation upon generation, people have read what the Poet saw and heard at the old pond; they see and hear it all anew, and many a reader comes away forever changed, marking a new day, a new life, from the reading of a book.

The Poet, of course, is Henry Thoreau, American transcendentalist writer (1817–1862), author of *Walden; Or, Life in the Woods* (1854), the classic work of American nature writing, who remains our culture's most thoughtful and influential observer of nature.

The Poet, of course, is Matsuo Bashō, Japanese writer of haiku, *haibun*, and renga (1644–1694), author of *The Narrow Road to the Deep North* (1694), the classic work of Japanese nature writing, who revolutionized the art of haiku, shaping it so as to accommodate plain and colloquial language with seriousness of purpose.

In my description of "the Poet" above, the pond is two ponds—Thoreau's Walden and Bashō's "old pond," subject of his most famous haiku, where he links the leap of a frog with "the sound of water." My ambiguous description of "the Poet" and his pond, lifting images, language, and themes from both Bashō and Thoreau, is meant to suggest that Bashō and Thoreau found something similar in their respective ponds, each managing to look past his own reflection to something deeper. Bashō preceded Thoreau by a century and a half, but we have no indication that Thoreau had any exposure to either Bashō's writing or the art of haiku. We do know that Thoreau was intensely interested in Eastern thought, but no haiku texts were available in nineteenth-century America, and so, not surprisingly, Thoreau never recorded in his voluminous journals any mention of Bashō or of haiku. But given the commonality of their ponds and their relations with the natural world, I am led to wonder: What if Thoreau had known of haiku? His view of the natural world, full of wonder, so hopeful of oneness, echoes the view so often expressed in the haiku tradition, as initiated by Bashō—so if we transpose Thoreau's language and observations of the natural world to the medium of haiku, would the content be compatible with the new form?

What follows is a venture into that world of "what if," a literary thought experiment. It will not take you long to figure out what I'm up to here—reducing *Walden*, chapter by chapter, to a series of haiku. I come to this project as an ecocritic who has long had an interest in the prose tradition of American nature writing—and who in recent years has become fascinated by the art of haiku. And yes, I see links between the two. It seems to me that the high points in nature writing are typically marked by those passages that contain the most haiku-like prose. Those high points are in essence "haiku moments," when the writer's awareness of self dissolves into egolessness, a dropping away of the boundaries between self and world such that what we get on the page is an attempt to place us in the world itself, as if the writer and her language were not even there intervening or mediating between us and the piece of the world under consideration. So partly this is an experiment to see if that trait of nature writing can be traced back—as so many of the important traits and themes of the nature-writing tradition can be—to *Walden*.

My curiosity regarding this topic was further aroused when my col-

league Sandy Petrulionis (editor of Thoreau's 1854 *Journal* for the Princeton edition), knowing of my interest in haiku, stopped by my office
one day and showed me Thoreau's journal entry for August 9, 1854:
"To Boston   Walden Published. Elder berries. Waxwork yellowing"
(8:259). "Just like a haiku," suggested Sandy, with the publication of
Walden juxtaposed with the ripening elderberries and fading waxwork
leaves (or "bittersweet," we call it these days)—not turning the elderberries or bittersweet into symbol, but simply allowing the two statements,
the affairs of the human world and the doings of the natural world, to
resonate with one another.

As it happens, such moments of resonance, akin to haiku, are not so
rare in Thoreau's writing. But first, allow me to issue a disclaimer: As I
note above, I'm not claiming that Thoreau was influenced by haiku or
even aware of haiku or the haiku tradition in writing *Walden*. I'm not
claiming that *Walden* itself constitutes some sort of extended haiku. I'm
not even claiming that *Walden* consistently and unerringly demonstrates
the traits of haiku. Clearly, Thoreau, in good transcendentalist fashion,
relies on metaphor a great deal (reading the physical world as a symbol
of spirit), in a way that haiku does not, eschewing as it does metaphor
in particular and figurative language in general in an attempt to see
nature on its own terms and not in terms of something else. Few readers
would claim for Thoreau's style the haiku ideals of "non-intellectuality"
or "wordlessness," or of the lightness of language that haiku poets call
karumi, and I have my doubts about how consistently he demonstrates
aware, the compassionate fellow feeling that permeates haiku—a compassion arising from the bittersweet realization and acceptance of the
impermanence of all things. Thoreau is certainly capable of compassion
for and identification with nonhuman animals (his "brute neighbors"),
but with other people . . . uh, not so much.

And yet, and yet—for all that, Thoreau's aesthetic principles and his
relationship with the natural world do turn out to have a great deal in
common with haiku. Let us count the ways: an emphasis on simplicity,
a respect for worn and humble and familiar things (*wabi*), a sense of
aloneness (*sabi*), a reliance on paradox, and the use of humor, especially

in the form of puns. Given all these resonances—and more, which I'll get to in due time—it is perhaps not so surprising that a reasonable abstract of the key themes and ideas of *Walden* can be produced by extracting from the text a series of Thoreau's haiku moments. With minimal editing, in order to make Thoreau's language conform to the formal expectations and traditions of haiku, I offer here a chapter-by-chapter redaction of *Walden* to a series of haiku. I couldn't quite get the whole book down to seventeen syllables or less, but I did manage an abridgement to 293 haiku. What becomes evident from such an attempt is that the most important ideas of *Walden* generally find expression in the most haiku-like language, language that relies on concrete diction and imagery, with frequent juxtaposition of images. The redaction to haiku, then, serves to abstract (ironically, in concrete form) key themes of the book—to put them in a tidier pile of nutshells. Further, the development of Thoreau's nature sensibility can be traced in his increasing reliance on haiku moments and haiku-like language and aesthetics as the book progresses. Applying the aesthetics of haiku gives us a new angle, a new vocabulary, and a new conceptual apparatus from which to view *Walden*, to understand Thoreau's purposes, and to appreciate his achievement. Reading *Walden* by haiku highlights the profound physicality of Thoreau's prose, and reveals a Walden Pond that is something more than a metaphoric surface where the self is reflected.

My purpose here, then, is threefold: to offer a primer on haiku, to provide fresh insights into *Walden*, and to demonstrate the pertinence of haiku aesthetics as a theoretical basis for understanding the nature-writing tradition in English.

In order to introduce the principles of haiku, in each section of part 1, adhering to the chapter-by-chapter arrangement of *Walden*, I first offer a series of haiku extracted from the text of *Walden*. The haiku are derived from moments of sharp, image-based perceptions, where the image—or, often, two or more juxtaposed images—suggests some depth of meaning and is packaged in interesting phrasing that is highlighted by being separated out from the text and given "featured" status as the gist of a stand-alone haiku. For the most part, the haiku follow the traditional three-line form of haiku in English. I have followed David Barnhill's practice (in *Bashō's Haiku*) of using "overlapping and indented lines, to suggest both the three-part rhythm and the continuity" of a traditional haiku (6). The wording, for the most part, is Thoreau's—with a few exceptions, I have tried to avoid changing or adding to his phrasings—but with many excisions and tense changes in order to make the resulting language conform to haiku conventions. Among those conventions (in English haiku) are the use of the present tense; a tight, noun-heavy free verse form of no more than seventeen syllables (and preferably less); an almost-exclusive reliance on simple diction and concrete imagery, with images often presented in juxtaposition; the absence of abstract diction or commentary or explanation; and the eschewing of figurative language. (This is hardly a complete list; for more, well, that's what the rest of the book will reveal!) Following the haiku drawn from each chapter of *Walden*, I offer a prose introduction to a principle of haiku aesthetics that seems especially pertinent to the subject or theme of the chapter. The haiku from "Solitude," for instance, lead to a discussion of *sabi*, or "aloneness," one of the qualities that contribute to haiku's poignancy.

Part 2, "Sources and Commentary," presents the source for each haiku in the original prose passage from *Walden*, followed by brief commentary on the individual haiku. Thus readers can see the context from which the haiku was drawn and perhaps gain some insight into the process of constructing haiku. The commentary following each passage points to the specific ways in which Thoreau's prose and worldview seem compatible with haiku aesthetics. If part 1 takes a macroscopic view, offering introductory and general ideas about haiku aesthetics to accompany the haiku extracted from *Walden*, part 2 is more microscopic in its analysis. At times the commentary elaborates on a principle of haiku aesthetics that seems pertinent to the haiku; at times it elaborates on a thematic or stylistic element of Thoreau's prose and its pertinence to haiku; and at still other times it illustrates the process of converting the prose into haiku, discussing the sorts of choices a haiku writer may face, in the act of composition, concerning what gets cut and why, and what might be the significance of what remains. At times, too, I confess to my own uncertainties, as shaper of the haiku, regarding whether the result sufficiently conforms to the conventions of haiku; many undoubtedly stray quite a bit. But I hope that revealing the process of composition and the occasional uncertainty about the result should convey to readers not yet familiar with haiku something of the challenges and satisfactions of writing in that form.

These prose passages may be read with the extracted haiku as a *haibun*, the combination of prose and haiku most famously presented in Bashō's classic *The Narrow Road to the Deep North*. Typically in a haibun there is a kind of echoing effect between the prose section and the haiku. That is, the haiku may echo a theme or the tonal quality of the prose passage. Sometimes the haiku picks up and elaborates on an image or word or phrase from the prose, though at times the haiku shifts tonal or thematic direction. For the most part, of course, one would obviously expect the haiku extracted from the text of *Walden* to echo the wording, theme, and tone of the original. By having access to the original passage, readers will be able to see for themselves the extent to which the haiku fairly represent the content and theme of the longer prose passage—and to get a sense of how haiku, while restricted primarily to pure image, manage to suggest larger dimensions of meaning. It is his confidence in the ability of the details of the natural world to resonate with significance that most links Thoreau with the writer of haiku.

Together the haiku drawn from *Walden*, the introduction of haiku aesthetic principles and thematic concerns in part 1, and the identification of source passages and analyses of individual haiku in part 2 make of Thoreau's classic work of nature writing a demonstration project on "how to haiku," a learning tool for anyone who might be interested in the art of haiku. Thoreau's prose can show us how clear and attentive and thoughtful description of the natural world—from American literature's master of such clear and attentive and thoughtful description—can be wrought into haiku. We have good reason to be interested in that process, since haiku has something important to teach us about human relations with the natural world—about how to nurture those relations, how to place ourselves in the world around us, and how to notice and appreciate it.

To the extent that *Walden by Haiku* serves as a primer on haiku, I count myself among the learners. This project started as a bit of a lark. I was asked to contribute to a panel on "Thoreau and Metaphor" at the American Literature Association Conference in San Francisco in 2005. Although much of my previous research and writing had focused on Thoreau, my recent research had been dedicated to haiku and not to Thoreau, so my first instinct was to beg off. But among its other pleasures, haiku teaches us to place and to notice things in juxtaposition. I was aware that many haiku writers had found inspiration in *Walden* and had seen in Thoreau a kindred spirit (see my commentary on these writers in "Reading")—even though he did not write any haiku and, as I have pointed out, we have no indication that he was familiar with the haiku tradition, which by Thoreau's day included its three most famous practitioners, Bashō, Buson, and Issa. What if Henry, out there by the old pond with the frogs jumping and the gentle sound of water set in motion, had known about and written haiku? I started playing around, thinking I'd find a few haiku-like moments embedded in the text and then could do a tidy little fifteen-minute presentation summarizing all of *Walden* in haiku form and adding some commentary about what Thoreau's life philosophy and writing style had in common with haiku (attention to nature, awareness of the seasons) and what it did not (his reliance on metaphor, which rarely finds a place in haiku).

I'll admit it—it was downright fun finding the haiku moments, and as I whittled and shaped Thoreau's language, trying to reveal the haiku within, trying to hone my own craft as a haiku poet, I felt like I was learning from a master. I was practicing the art of simplifying, simplifying, from many words to the vital few, by starting with the raw material of the prose I most admire. Like many admirers of Thoreau as stylist, I had often wondered, upon reading his journal, how it was possible for someone to write so beautifully, so thoughtfully, so powerfully, every day of his adult life. Haiku is the essence of poetry, and finding the poetry in

Thoreau's prose turned out to be thoroughly gratifying, partly because I rarely had to look long or far to find the next haiku image. I am reminded of the story William Ellery Channing tells about a companion asking Thoreau how he managed to find so many arrowheads. Thoreau said, Why, they're all around, and just then he stooped to pick one up at his feet. The eye, it seems, sees only what it is prepared to see. Or as Thoreau puts it in "Autumnal Tints," "We cannot see anything until we are possessed with the idea of it, take it into our heads,—and then we can hardly see anything else" (136–37). So it happened with the haiku of *Walden*. Once I started looking, I found hundreds, ultimately rejected many that seemed to lack depth or resonance or sufficient precision of image, and ended up with the 293 presented here.

Perhaps the process by which I extracted haiku-like images and language from the text of *Walden* deserves further explanation. First, I went through the text chapter by chapter and started arranging the phrases with strong images as haiku. After an initial run through the text, I had collected about twice as many haiku as I ended up with. The eliminated candidates, the ones that seemed less successful as haiku, often had adequate images but didn't seem to go anywhere or to suggest anything particularly meaningful—that is, they lacked the depth of meaning and resonance that in haiku is called *yūgen* (fittingly pronounced "you gain"). In some other cases I eliminated an epigrammatic statement that said something important thematically, especially in terms of thinking of this project as a synopsis-of-*Walden*-by-haiku, but that lacked a strong enough image.

I fully admit to the subjective vagaries of my procedure. It is possible that in reviewing some chapters I may have felt less creative that day or been less alert and attentive, and undoubtedly some fine potential haiku slipped past me. Or I may have tried and failed to make a decent haiku out of some promising material, and the resulting haiku may have been weeded out during the editing process. But still, I think the end product, subjective as it may be, indicates some broad general trends in the text of *Walden*, suggesting where Thoreau's senses and intuition become his primary means of engaging with the world around Walden Pond.

So what did I learn at the feet of haiku master Henry? The answer to that leads me to my second purpose, for what one can glean from Thoreau about writing haiku highlights dimensions of Thoreau's writing style that we may not have previously noticed. To put it in a nutshell: as a writer of haiku, as a reader of *Walden*, I have come to appreciate more than ever Thoreau's practice of combining close attention to details of the natural world ("We live amid surfaces," says Emerson in "Experience," "and the true art of life is to skate well on them" [35]) with stylistic verve and deep resonances of meaning. I was already aware that haiku presents quiet observations about nature in concrete details, and that it should add up to some depth of meaning worth pondering. The meaningfulness is often conveyed by the blank part of the page surrounding the few suggestive words of the haiku, its content only implied, left unstated, maybe not capable of being expressed in language, or not needing to be. These haiku elements, as I say, I was previously aware of. But working with *Walden* highlighted for me the appeal of stylistic quirks in the phrasing of a haiku—the sound devices and rhythms, Thoreau's sheer playfulness with language, the puns and paradoxes and startling word choices. I am reminded that the *hai* in haiku means "humor." Of course, the humor is not simply the quick tee-hee of mock-philosophical "pseudohaiku" about things like computer problems and being stuck in traffic. Haiku poet and critic Lee Gurga notes that these "zappai," as he calls them, reflect—and engender—widespread misunderstanding about the nature of haiku (*Haiku* 127–28). The real thing may be humorous, and haiku can certainly be light in tone, but there is also something serious and thought-provoking, some insight, below the surface and beyond the image. That's the part of a haiku written on the blank part of the page.

When I look at many contemporary haiku written in English, and at my own haiku prior to engaging in this project, I see an overemphasis on concreteness and plainness of language such that there is a kind of flatness in the voice and at times a lack of further dimension. Precision of image, it seems, is prized at the expense of sound, verbal play, or resonance. But Thoreau manages a kind of language that, while it focuses intently on images—to an even greater extent than I had noticed in all my previous readings of *Walden*—at the same time employs striking turns of phrase, full of serious puns and interesting rhythms and, often, uses of alliteration and assonance. These traits account for the wonderful sound of Thoreau's prose and its aptness for highlighting in the form of haiku. But besides their ear appeal, Thoreau's images are eminently worth pondering, often layered, often pointing us toward a region of intellectual richness. There is *dimension* in Thoreau's language. At random, I open my copy of *Walden*, and I come to this line from "The Pond in Winter": "Then to my morning work. First I take an axe and pail and go in search of water, if that be not a dream" (282). It's such simple description, that second line full of monosyllabic words but for the two-syllable *water*. But it's also very rhythmic—look, listen, it's almost perfectly iambic. But for all its simplicity, in a book filled with references to awakening and promises of "more day to dawn," we know that "morning work" is something so positive as to be sanctified. And what is it that is sanctified? Physical labor, for starters—Thoreau's affection for work with his hands is suggested by the mention of axe and pail. The image suggests the pleasure of doing daily chores, of getting one's living. And his work takes him to the pond, "pure and deep for a symbol," the book's most prominent symbol of all the purity and depth Thoreau finds in the natural world. The water he seeks, first thing in his new day, is the most basic necessity of life, but it also partakes of the ethereal stuff of dream.

This is just to say that Thoreau's prose works as haiku because the language is sharp, imagistic, and interesting (sometimes startlingly so); it is attentive to natural details; it sounds good; and it is meaningful. Taking the time for a microscopic reading of *Walden* repays the attention of those who admire both Thoreau and haiku. The fact that Thoreau's prose lends itself to haiku suggests a connection in terms of shared subject matter, if not a direct influence. Reading *Walden* through the lens of haiku aesthetics allows us to see it in a new light and with new appreciation. The process of winnowing Thoreau's prose in search of haiku moments and images, of lingering over his images, phrases, and sentences, letting them sink in, often revealed to me a pun I'd previously passed over, or the sheer aptness, precision, and depth of a word choice or image. I was struck too by how well Thoreau's images withstand being processed into metaphor without being drained of their vitality or subsumed by the metaphor. I had previously read and taught *Walden* a couple of dozen times, yet in the process of seeking out haiku-like images and phrases, I found myself startled by the frequency of new discoveries of nuance and detail in Thoreau's words. Is it a new *Walden* I present here? No, I would not claim that—but haiku teaches us to notice and appreciate anew what is old and familiar to us.

In applying haiku aesthetics to *Walden*, I was also surprised to discover just how neatly the aesthetic principles of haiku could be applied to the text—that's one reason the project changed from a short presentation to a book. The tidy fit seemed like it must be more than coincidence, and that started me thinking in larger terms. Ecocriticism is a fairly new sort of literary-critical endeavor, especially if we date its birth to the formation of the Association for the Study of Literature and Environment (ASLE) in 1992, and it has certainly benefited from the enthusiasm of its youth as its practitioners have excitedly latched on to the promise of a new approach to familiar texts and the rediscovery and revaluing of the whole rich genre of nature writing, in all its forms. But increasingly we hear the quibbles and questions: Is there really an ecocritical methodology or theory, or is ecocriticism simply an attitude that borrows from other modes of literary criticism and happens to focus on literary works that feature natural settings? Is ecocriticism nothing more than literary criticism that happens to focus on the place of environment in literature, or is there something distinctive about an ecocritical approach? Similarly, we might wonder if there is such a thing as a nature-writing aesthetics, or if nature writing is simply writing that happens to focus on nature. To some of us, it certainly seems qualitatively different, but there has not been much of an attempt to explore its uniqueness, at least not beyond the observation that nature writing and ecocriticism share an interest in ecological values.

But if nature writing has seemed to lack its own aesthetics and ecocriticism its theoretical and methodological principles, well, haiku has not. There is in fact a well-developed aesthetics of haiku that dates back hundreds of years, a ready-made set of aesthetics that, I contend, can be fruitfully applied to nature writing as part of an ecocritical approach. Among these are concepts derived from Japanese literary aesthetics, many of them dating back to Bashō's revolution in haiku practice in the late 1600s. Some quick examples: *hosomi*, or slenderness; *karumi*, or lightness; *wabi*, or appreciation for poverty and simplicity; *sabi*, or aloneness; *aware*, or compassion arising from the recognition of the impermanence of all things; and *shibumi*, or astringency. Other aesthetic tenets can be traced back to R. H. Blyth's enormously influential four-volume *Haiku* (1949–52) and his two-volume *History of Haiku* (1963–64), the books that are perhaps most responsible for bringing awareness of the haiku tradition to the West and for initiating the development of a Western haiku tradition. Blyth identified thirteen attributes of haiku: selflessness, loneliness, grateful acceptance, wordlessness, non-intellectuality, contradiction, humor, freedom, non-morality, simplicity, materiality, love, and courage. These are still regarded by Western haiku writers and critics as decent starting points for haiku aesthetics.

Walden by Haiku can serve, I hope, as a demonstration of how those aesthetic principles can be applied to a classic work of Western nature writing. But it seems reasonable to believe that Thoreau's prose, as influential as it has been in the American nature-writing tradition, is not alone in its compatibility with the borrowed aesthetics of haiku. Like haiku, nature writing (by which I mean both the nonfiction tradition of writing about place and fiction and poetry that are environmentally focused and aware) is marked by the presence of epiphanic moments of connection, where the writer's intense awareness of the world around him or her seems to obliterate, temporarily, the perceiver's awareness of self—at least an awareness of self as something separate from the world around the perceiver. Like haiku, nature writing shifts attention from the individual perceiver to the natural world. Ecocritics, borrowing from deep ecologists, have recognized this tendency and privileged it in the concept of "ecocentrism," where the egocentric self is replaced by the

ecocentric self. Like haiku, nature writing typically privileges simplicity and solitude.[1] If nature writing has in common with haiku a set of
themes and stylistic and rhetorical practices—and I hope to demonstrate
through the example of Thoreau that it does—then ecocritics interested
in that tradition stand to benefit from the established set of critical and
analytical tools available in haiku aesthetics.

The process of converting *Walden* into haiku, then, serves as a primer
on haiku, a way to highlight elements of Thoreau's craft as a writer and
of his nature philosophy, and finally as an introduction to aesthetic
principles, drawn from the haiku realm, that may be pertinent to an
understanding of the Western nature-writing tradition. But perhaps this
introduction is an appropriate place to confess to some of the creative
and scholarly dilemmas I found myself considering as I engaged in this
process. Problem number one involves the issue of theft and cultural appropriation. Haiku is a literary form and an aesthetic tradition associated
with Japanese cultural values, so what in the world is gained by applying
all that to a classic of the American literary tradition? And more to the
point: What of the source tradition is lost or compromised or diminished?
If those questions weren't enough to trouble my conscience, I could add
to my list of pilfered goods the very words and phrases and images lifted
from the pages of *Walden*. Considering the high regard in which I hold
both the Japanese haiku tradition and the writings of Henry Thoreau, I
admit to thinking twice and thrice about my many borrowings.

To address first the question of cultural appropriation: It is true that
the haiku form has its origins in Japan, dating back over a thousand years
to the elegant form of *waka*, a verse form of five phrases, consisting of
sound units per phrase in the following sequence: 5–7–5–7–7. *Waka*
spawned the communal verse form of *renga*, where several poets would
add pieces together to form a chain of *waka*-like poems. A renga would
begin with an opening hokku of 5–7–5; then the next poet would add
phrases of 7–7, forming one *waka*-like poem. Then the next would take
the previous phrases of 7–7 and add another cluster of 5–7–5, to form another poem, and so on, to a total of thirty-six or one hundred verse pieces.
By Bashō's day, the form had become a little more colloquial, combining

some earthy humor with a spiritual quality, and had become known as *haikai no renga*. Bashō, then, was a *haikai* poet, but one renowned for writing particularly striking hokku. The term *haiku*, combining *hokku* and *haikai*, was the creation of the more recent great poet Shiki, writing in the late nineteenth and early twentieth centuries—just before haiku began to become known in the West.

OK, so clearly the origins of haiku are in Japan. Therefore, to apply aesthetic principles derived from that long literary tradition to a writer who never even heard of haiku or haikai or hokku might seem peculiar at best and the essence of cultural appropriation at worst. But though haiku's origins are clearly Japanese, there has also developed in the past half century a thriving English-language tradition. There are quite a few excellent haiku journals in North America, foremost among them, perhaps, *Frogpond* and *Modern Haiku*. These and other journals feature a number of superb haiku poets, or *haijin*, and a body of criticism dedicated to the form, with lots of commentary on how the Western haiku tradition can translate the formal qualities of haiku to the English language (or other European languages) and how haiku can meld or balance or incorporate both Western and Eastern cultural traditions. In short, the form is no longer exclusively Japanese, and the aesthetic ideas that may have originated in reference to the Japanese tradition have already been demonstrated to have some value in the more recent Western tradition. This has not been a process of appropriation or even wholesale adoption of aesthetic principles; rather, it has been a process of *adaptation* of those principles, and that is what I suggest could be helpful in exploring how these aesthetic ideas might pertain to works from the Western nature-writing tradition.

There is a reason, of course, why the haiku form has appealed to so many in the West in the last half century. The haiku tradition offers a literary form and an aesthetics that seems not only vital to us now, but also compatible with the alternative story that the nature-writing tradition has been telling us all along about our place in the world. I would also hope that readers who are interested in the pertinence of haiku aesthetics to the Western nature-writing tradition would in turn be inspired to become readers (and writers) of haiku. I'm not interested in conflating the two cultures, whether social or literary, or in absorbing one into the other. Rather, I am interested in the possibilities of creative engagement across cultures.

The question of what I owe Thoreau by way of credit or apology has also troubled my conscience more than a few times during the process of redacting *Walden* to a series of haiku. But beyond any crisis of conscience I experienced, those questions raise, I think, some interesting theoretical issues concerning the source of these haiku. Did I write them, or did Thoreau? When I claim to have found these haiku in the text, does that mean they were somehow present there in the text, or is the finding really more a product of my own imposition of the haiku form onto Thoreau's unsuspecting text? Are the haiku taken from the text really a product of my own mind, prepared to see the haiku in *Walden* only because I happen to have been reading lots of haiku journals?

These questions quickly get us to some central questions about literature and the perception of meaning. Where is meaning found? Is it the product of the author's intent? Is it found in the text? Or is it a creation of the reader? Can we cop out and say all of the above?

I'm tempted to reject the first possibility for the source of the haiku — author's intent — out of hand. After all, since the days of New Criticism we have learned to consider such a claim the "intentional fallacy," recognizing that we can never really have access to an author's intent. Beyond that theoretical objection is a more practical one. Obviously Thoreau, being unaware of the haiku tradition, could not be deliberately fashioning haiku-like language or looking at the world in some manner explicitly informed by the way of haiku. True enough. But in trying to see the world as it is, to come to know it through direct experience, to inquire into the meaning and value of a natural fact, to wonder what it means "to live deliberately," Thoreau indeed had to have in mind (some of) these intentions and to have pursued them deliberately, in a way that suggests some convergent evolution between Thoreau at Walden and the writer of haiku. It may be in fact part of Thoreau's intention to privilege pure image, the things themselves of the natural world, in such

a fashion as to suggest the depth of meaning inherent in the simple presentation of natural objects, a depth of meaning by which every natural
detail bespeaks its own nature and its place in the larger context of the
seasons.

In speaking of Thoreau's privileging of pure image and his ability to
combine image with meaning, I am gauging Thoreau's intent based on
what can be found in the comfortable New Critical terrain of the text.
It is an easier contention that the haiku found here are implicit in the
text, just as the arrowheads that Thoreau went looking for really were
there in the ground. It's not such a stretch to contend that the text of
Walden (and likely the texts of other writers in the nature-writing tradition since Thoreau) seems remarkably haiku-like in some regards, and
so Thoreau's prose lends itself to haiku treatment. What features of the
text seem haiku-like? In sum, the selection of images, often juxtaposed,
where the physical images can carry a large freight of meaning and can
convey resonance and depth—those images being presented in language
interesting enough to arrest our attention—all of which highlights an
intensely meaningful moment of perception in the space of a haiku's
"breath unit." In this sense I contend that the haiku moments are latent
in the text, waiting to be "found" or unearthed or brought to our attention, and I contend that haiku aesthetics can help us better understand
what is going on in *Walden*. Thoreau's prose indeed evinces the spirit
and techniques of haiku such that despite the vast difference of cultural
origins, we can speak, to some extent at least, of a shared worldview, a
world in which seasonal change is the focal point and where the writer
aims to make the natural world fully present and meaningful. In my
conclusion I suggest that a whole vein of the American nature-writing
tradition may be similarly compatible with the aesthetics of haiku, and so
literary ecocritics might find that long-standing body of aesthetic theory
useful in reading and understanding their subject.

On the other hand (I think I'm on the third hand now, that of the
reader), just as any "found" poetry results as much from the selection
process of the seeker and finder as it does from the inherent quality
of the source writing, I admit that the found haiku presented here are

at least in part the product of my own imagination. I found haiku in Thoreau's prose precisely because I went looking for them and because I was prepared to see them from my reading—just as Thoreau had to prepare his mind's eye to find arrowheads.

Ultimately, I don't want to insist too much on any one answer to the question of just where the haiku moments I discovered in Thoreau's text come from—Henry, the text itself, or this particular quirky reader, who happens to have juxtaposed, haiku-like, two images of literary excellence. But even if this project bends the subjective branch of reader-response theory (the School of Fish, it has been called, in honor—or not—of Stanley Fish), I would still hope that there is something of interest here to all readers in offering a fresh look at a much-studied classic. If every reading of a literary work is a new text that is in part the creation of a reader, well, we can never have too many *Waldens*. Here's one I bet you haven't heard before.

PART ONE

Walden by Haiku

Economy

farms, houses, barns, cattle —
    easily acquired
        hard to get rid of

                serfs of the soil
                  digging their graves
                    as soon as they are born

compost
    the better part of a man
        ploughed into the soil

                the oxen
                  their vegetable-made bones
                  the lumbering plough

ripens my beans
    illumines a system of earths
        the same sun

a seed
    rooted firmly in the earth
      rising to the heavens

           long ago lost
              a hound, a horse, and a dove
                I am still on their trail

trying to hear
    what is in the wind
      I lose my own breath

           the cornice of the palace
             finished—the mason
               returns to his hut

limestone on my desk
    dusted daily
      no dust gathers on the grass

           a borrowed axe
            returned
             sharper

a striped snake
　　lying still in the pond
　　　　as long as I stay there

　　　　　　　　more friend than foe
　　　　　　　cutting the pines
　　　　　　　　　becoming better acquainted

no curtains
　　no gazers to shut out
　　　but the sun and the moon

What better point to initiate a discussion of haiku aesthetics than "economy"? If haiku is the essence of poetry, economy is the essence of haiku. Make do with less, make less count for more, make every word count. In haiku the concept of *hosomi*, usually translated as "spareness" or "slenderness" or "underemphasis," is roughly equivalent to Thoreau's economy. The spareness and slenderness are readily apparent in a poetic form featuring such economy of expression—so few words, such simple words, so little explanation. Whatever else may be going on that is not immediately apparent, a haiku looks slight on the page. But in haiku the emphasis on spareness refers not only to the scaled-down form and language but also to the idea being expressed. Is spareness not the essence of Thoreau's thought? "Shall we always study to obtain more of these things," he asks, "and not sometimes to be content with less?" (36). His "greatest skill," he claims, "has been to want but little"

(69). He speaks of "that economy of living which is synonymous with philosophy" (52).

One critic translates *hosomi* as "underemphasis" (Giroux 111). It is debatable, perhaps, whether the language of "Economy" stands as a great example of that quality of underemphasis. If anything, Thoreau seems to protest too much, and to explain too much. I am mindful of students who find Thoreau too preachy, obnoxiously so, arrogant even. My impression is that readers either identify with Thoreau and find him speaking for them against the evils and stupidities and superficialities of our culture—or they feel themselves targeted or accused by him and are thereby put off by him. Either way, his position regarding the need for a philosophy of economy is hardly presented in an underemphatic way. But "Economy" is where Thoreau lays out the philosophical basis for the book—and for his way of life as well. Taking up a third of the book's volume, the chapter is itself not exactly a model of economy. But by outlining Thoreau's philosophy of life, the opening chapter prepares us to understand the underemphasized descriptions of the natural world that appear later in the book.

Take, for example, Thoreau's description of the garter snake in torpor, resting on the bottom of the pond, one of the relatively few strong natural images from this long chapter. Immediately after presenting this image, Thoreau draws the philosophical moral: "It appeared to me that for a like reason men remain in their present low and primitive condition; but if they should feel the influence of the spring of springs arousing them, they would of necessity rise to a higher and more ethereal life" (41). This, of course, is classic transcendental method, the natural fact leading to the very-much-emphasized spiritual or moral lesson. But later in the book we get the images without the morals drawn for us—they are left for us to pursue or perceive or not, but either way the moral no longer receives the same emphasis as it does here. Lee Gurga says of hosomi that it "allows the poet to paint the scene, then disappear" (126). In "Economy" Thoreau emphatically establishes his presence, but what he learns over the course of his seasons at Walden is to cultivate the state of egolessness that hosomi makes possible, and the images later in the book tend to be presented with greater restraint and underemphasis.

Thoreau's strong personality, as it is being established in "Economy," suggests another principle of haiku aesthetics: *shibumi*. The term can suggest the asceticism implicit in the idea of "economy," but it is more frequently translated as "astringency." That quality, says Gurga, "gives haiku its tang—the flavor of persimmons rather than peaches" (126). Me, I think of wild berries as opposed to domesticated ones, like the blueberries with a "smart and spicy taste" that Thoreau admired so much on Mt. Katahdin ("Ktaadn" 71). And Thoreau's persona established in "Economy" is like that—astringent, a little severe, a little sour—the man some readers find arrogant and scolding and hard to take. It's that cantankerous "I" introduced in the first few paragraphs of *Walden*, who says, "I should not talk so much about myself if there were any body else whom I knew as well. Unfortunately, I am confined to this theme by the narrowness of my experience" (3). The reference to the "narrowness" of his experience is a joke, of course, since Thoreau truly believes his experience of life has been much richer and deeper than that of his fellow citizens. But the reference is also true, in the sense of the slenderness of hosomi—the richness of his life is centered on little things like picking huckleberries and building his own cabin and chopping wood and chasing loons and walking over the frozen pond. What makes his account "astringent" is the lack of sentimentality in his writing or in his way of life. There is a quality of restraint that becomes more and more evident over the course of the book and the passage of the seasons.

Where I Lived, and What I Lived For

the landscape retained
its yield carried off
without a wheelbarrow

chanticleer in the morning
standing on his roost
waking the neighbors

the pond's soft ripples
morning mists
withdrawing to the woods

the wood-thrush heard
from shore to shore
the lake never smoother

the earth beyond the pond
a thin crust
floating

religious exercise
I get up early
and bathe in the pond

a mosquito
touring the cabin at dawn
singing its wrath

an honest man
counting on his fingers
adding his toes

the sleepers
that underlie the rails
sound sleepers, I assure you

thrown off the track
a mosquito's wing
on the rails

drinking deeper from the stream
fish in the sky
bottom pebbly with stars

Clearly what Thoreau lived for has a whole lot in common with what haiku tries to convey. Actually, the first two chapters of *Walden*, "Economy" and "Where I Lived, and What I Lived For," are lighter in haiku moments, at least on a per-page basis, than the rest of the book. That's not surprising, really, since it is in these opening chapters that Thoreau lays out much of his theory and philosophy of life, and statements of theory and philosophy are antithetical to the concrete language and outward-looking nature of haiku. But Thoreau's statements of philosophy serve not only to define his life in the woods but also to echo the aesthetic principles and worldview of haiku. One of those key principles is the concept of *wabi*, literally "desolation" or "poverty," referring to the idea that material poverty is a necessary precondition for spiritual richness. To wit, quoting haiku master Henry: "Most of the luxuries, and many of the so-called comforts of life, are not only not indispensable, but positive hinderances to the elevation of mankind. With respect to luxuries and comforts, the wisest have ever lived a more simple and meager life than the poor" (14). Or as Richard Powell puts it, wabi refers to "the ideal hermit's life, lived in contemplation of nature and appreciation of the spiritual and aesthetic values underlying a solitary existence" (6). He could be describing Thoreau at Walden.

Wabi accounts for haiku's focus on familiar, worn, simple, ordinary things, "the understated and unrefined," says Powell (7), and what Thoreau says about food, clothing, and shelter all qualify as such. Thoreau's warning to "beware of all enterprises that require new clothes" is another way of reminding us to prefer simplicity and to return to the old, worn, and familiar, for "A man who has at length found something to do will not need to get a new suit to do it in" (23). Thoreau applies to food this same preference for the simple and familiar. For twenty-seven cents a week, he lives on bread with no yeast, "potatoes, rice, salt pork, molasses, and salt, and my drink water" (60). And we could point to just about any passage in Thoreau's extended discussion of shelter to see further examples of a wabi aesthetic. To choose just one: "The most interesting dwellings in this country, as the painter knows, are the most unpretending, humble log huts and cottages of the poor commonly; it is the life of the inhabitants whose shells they are . . . which makes them *picturesque*; and equally interesting will be the citizen's suburban box, when his life shall be as simple and as agreeable to the imagination, and there is as little straining after effect in the style of his dwelling" (47).

Besides summing up Thoreau's worldview, the concept of "economy" can also serve as a statement of haiku aesthetics. It's a philosophy not so much of "less is more" as "less is all you need." Or, as he famously puts it in "Where I Lived, and What I Lived For": "Simplify, simplify" (91). Simple language to describe ordinary things—that is basic to haiku, as is the focus on the natural world. "Let us spend one day as deliberately as Nature" (97), urges Thoreau—and the practitioner of haiku. Toward the end of "Where I lived, and What I Lived For," Thoreau says, "I have always been regretting that I was not as wise as the day I was born" (98). Here he offers the ideal of beginner's mind, the attempt to see the world at every moment as if you are seeing it for the first time, to let go of preconceptions. These are starting points for haiku practice.

Reading

Iliad on the table
my house to finish
my beans to hoe

reading books of travel
I ask where it was
that *I* lived

writing and speech
the firmament with its stars
behind the clouds

there are the stars
and they who can
may read them

books
the oldest and best
stand on the shelves

man weathercocks
swinging round there
till they are rusty

the hired man
and Zoroaster
travelling the same road

Given the topic of this chapter, it may be pertinent to note what other readers have made of the connection between Thoreau and haiku, for both practitioners and critics of haiku have certainly sensed a connection. R. H. Blyth first popularized haiku in North America with his four-volume study *Haiku* (the source of the Beats' discovery of haiku). His presentation of "Eastern Culture" in the first volume features frequent quotes from Thoreau that help convey what Blyth saw as the Zen underpinnings of haiku.[2] Robert Spiess, the former editor of the journal *Modern Haiku*, continued the tradition in his "Speculations" on haiku that appeared regularly in *Modern Haiku*. Spiess offers five quotes from Thoreau for writers of haiku to keep in mind. The first, commenting on the seasons as the most prominent subject of haiku, is this: "It is in vain to write on the seasons unless you have the seasons in you." The second, referring to haiku's primary appeal to intuition: "The intellect should never speak; it is not a natural sound." Third, evoking the idea that haiku should treat familiar things in nature but make them seem startlingly fresh: "All the phenomena of nature need to be seen from the point of view of wonder and awe, like lightning; and on the other hand, the lightning itself needs to be regarded with serenity, as the most familiar and innocent phenomena are." Fourth, stressing haiku's focus on the familiar: "My themes shall not be far-fetched. I will tell of homely every-day phenomena" (qtd. in "What Is Haiku?"). And finally, focusing on the idea that haiku's subject is the present moment in all its fullness: "You must live in the present, launch yourself on any wave, find your eternity in each moment" (qtd. in "Definitions"). This is just to say that Spiess and Blyth recognized that Thoreau's aesthetic principles and worldview share common ground with haiku.

That common ground is the basis for Mary Kullberg's 1993 book, *Morning Mist: Through the Seasons with Matsuo Basho and Henry David Thoreau*. This season-based collection compares Bashō's haiku to some of Thoreau's more mystical-sounding and image-making phrases. Kullberg's point is to highlight Bashō's and Thoreau's shared attunement to the seasons and to a spirit of mind and soul and language that pays close attention to the natural world. Unlike me, she doesn't alter Thoreau's words to make them fit haiku patterns—just reprints the words verbatim, though with occasional arrangements in three lines (but not condensed). For example, Bashō's haiku "I clap my hands / and with the echoes the day begins— / the summer moon" is compared to these lines by Thoreau:

> I used to strike with a paddle on the side of my boat
> . . . filling the woods with circling and dilating sound,
> awakening the woods. (58)

That's faithful to Thoreau's words but rather long-winded for a haiku. My renderings of Thoreau's prose are typically less faithful to his words and more guided by the constraints of haiku. But like Kullberg, I too sense there's something of the haiku artist inherent in Thoreau.

More recently, in an essay called "Thoreau and the Haiku Spirit," Cor van den Heuvel has pointed to the presence of "haiku-like brief vignettes" and the "objective" quality of Thoreau's prose in selecting passages from "Walking" and *Walden* as "perfect" examples of haibun (again, haibun is a blend of haiku and prose, sometimes a kind of travel writing, often poetically charged) (55–58). Van den Heuvel also points out that Thoreau's practice of revision has much in common with haiku practice, in that his "revisions often took the form of deleting things"— thus paring things (such as ideas, descriptions, or a life) down to their essence (59).

The most extensive treatment of Thoreau in the context of haiku is Tom Lynch's unpublished doctoral dissertation, "An Original Relation to the Universe: Haiku, Zen, and the American Literary Tradition." Lynch traces the links between Eastern philosophy and Thoreau's, finding them to be the result not so much of influence (though Thoreau was familiar with the *Bhagavad Gita*) as "convergent evolution," and he posits that, because of the shared worldview between the transcendentalists and Eastern ideas, "a poetry very much like haiku, and perhaps even a philosophy very much like Zen, would have developed on this continent independently of any direct contact with Buddhism or Japanese literature" (55).

I don't mean to belabor the point that I am not the first to notice a connection between Thoreau's philosophy and the aesthetic principles of haiku. Nor am I the first to repackage Thoreau's words as haiku. There seems to be a tradition, dating back to Blyth, of mining the work of English-language poets for haiku gems. In addition to a couple from *A Week*, Blyth offers this one from *Walden*: "Turn to the old; / Things do not change, / We change" (Blyth 308). More recently Peter Washington has edited a collection of haiku, part of the Everyman's Library Pocket Poets series, that includes classic haiku from Japanese masters like Bashō, Buson, Issa, and Shiki, as well as excerpts from Thoreau and other English-language poets (namely Wordsworth, Keats, Tennyson, and Hopkins) put into haiku form.[3]

In short, others before me have already suggested that Thoreau's prose and philosophy have something in common with haiku. What I hope to add to the conversation is further development and illustration, identifying specific phrasing and images that can be converted to haiku form and noting specific links between the aesthetic principles of haiku and the philosophy of life espoused in *Walden*.

Perhaps even more so than scholars, haiku poets themselves have sensed that they have something to learn about their craft from Thoreau.

The highly regarded haiku poet Vincent Tripi's first book, *Haiku Pond*, intersperses some of Thoreau's journal entries among his own haiku. Of course, the title too suggests the extent of Thoreau's influence. In effect, Tripi reenacts the Thoreauvian experiment by living by the side of a pond (Tripi's is in New Hampshire) in order to discover something about the essence of life—and then writing about the experience. Haiku and Thoreau are two lenses that clarify his vision in terms of helping him see life's essence.

Here are two more haiku that, in the tradition of allusion in haiku (or *honkadori*), evoke Thoreau's spirit:

> Thoreau's gravesite:
> the smell of woodsmoke
> on the cold spring air
> —Bruce Ross (van den Heuvel, *Haiku Anthology* 167)

> lighting the path
> to Walden Pond—
> my bedside lamp
> —Ebba Story (van den Heuvel, *Haiku Anthology* 207)

In Ross's haiku, Thoreau's gravestone and the wood smoke serve as nonauditory echoes of one another, both evoking the memory of Henry. Story's haiku suggests that *Walden* accomplishes the goal of a good haiku: it is no longer a bunch of words about the pond, but the pond itself. The words have disappeared, ceasing to mediate between the observer and the place being described. What is left is the place itself, Walden Pond. Reading *Walden*, Story is at Walden. The book and the pond are no longer two separate things. This is the haiku ideal of "wordlessness," where language becomes so simple, so transparent, it is as if there is no language at all interceding between the reader and the piece of the world being presented.

Sounds

much published, little printed
    the rays which stream
        through the shutters

            a broad margin
                from sunrise till noon
                    my doorway

a traveller's wagon
    the distant highway
        corn growing in the night

            it was morning, and lo,
                now it is evening
                    incessant good fortune

furniture on the grass
    white sand and water
        scrubbing the cabin floor

three-legged table
    books and pen and ink
        standing amid the pines

                        a bird on the next bough
                            life-everlasting grows
                                under the table

hawks circling
    tantivy of wild pigeons
        giving voice to the air

                    rattle of railroad cars
                        dying and reviving
                            the beat of a partridge

along the rail line
    a track-repairer
        the orbit of the earth

the locomotive whistle
penetrates my woods
the scream of a hawk

timber on a freight train
the country hands a chair
to the city

freight train
cranberry meadows
raked into the city

iron horse
the hills echo
the earth shakes

the rising of the sun
clouds stretching to heaven
train going to Boston

farmers' clocks
set to the train whistle
keeping track of time

an echo
of the Concord bell
partly the voice of the wood

the evening train gone by
whippoorwills
chanting their vespers

screech owls
their ancient u-lu-lu
oh that I never had been born

owls
let them do the hooting
for men

evening
the trump of bullfrogs
trying to sing a catch

frog tr-r-r-oonk
round again and again
that there be no mistake

a winter morning
cockerels crow clear and shrill
the earth resounding

in the Great Snow
no path to the front-yard gate
no gate—no front yard

Interesting—"Sounds" has, according to my findings, the most haiku moments of any chapter so far (twenty-four), more than any other until we get to the last two, "Spring" and "Conclusion" (with thirty-one and twenty-nine, respectively). The last two chapters, perhaps, indicate where Thoreau is heading: more and more in touch with nature, with less and less ego-consciousness intervening. But then why so many haiku moments here in "Sounds," relatively early in the narrative? They demonstrate, I think, an important shift. Thus far Thoreau has been more or less philosophical, living in the mind as much as he is living by the pond. Here he makes the break with tradition—the tradition of intellectualism and rational justification for why he chose the radical path of going to the woods to live. Now it's time for pure being. One of the Zen qualities that R. H. Blyth identifies as essential to haiku is this sort of "non-intellectuality," the movement away from conceptualizing the world to perceiving it.

Tellingly, it is in this chapter, right after he has been preoccupied with "Reading," that Thoreau gives us this declaration, which could fit comfortably in any statement of haiku aesthetics: "We are in danger of forgetting the language which all things and events speak without metaphor . . . What is a course of history, or philosophy, or poetry, no matter how well selected, or the best society . . . compared with the discipline of looking always at what is to be seen?"(111). To that we might add, apropos of this chapter, and "listening always to what is to be heard." Note how the passive construction here ("at what is to be seen") takes the emphasis off the perceiver and places it on the thing perceived: not "what I see" but "what is to be seen," with an implied erasure, for the moment at least, of the first person. One of haiku's first principles is that it looks outward at the natural world, not inward at the self. Here in "Sounds" is where *Walden*'s shift to outward things is most dramatically marked.

Solitude

a delicious evening
the whole body
one sense

over the water
note of the whippoorwill
borne on the rippling wind

fluttering alder leaves
take away my breath
the lake not ruffled

dark now
the wind still roars
the waves still dash

calling cards
a willow wand, a name in pencil
on a yellow leaf

a traveller
along the highway
the scent of his pipe

the woods and the pond
the horizon
never quite at our elbows

my own sun and moon and stars
and a little world
all to myself

fishing for pouts
baiting the hooks
with darkness

why should I feel lonely?
is not our planet
in the Milky Way?

I am driftwood in the stream
Indra in the sky
looking down on it

the student at his desk
at work in his field
chopping in his woods

we meet at meals
a new taste
of that old musty cheese

no more lonely
than the loon in the pond
or the pond itself

Walden Pond
the blues
in the tint of its waters

dandelion in a pasture
the north star
the south wind

intelligence with the earth
myself partly leaves
and vegetable mould

a draught of morning air!
it will not keep
quite till noon

Another of the defining characteristics of haiku is *sabi*, which roughly translates as "aloneness" or, as Sam Hamill has called it, "existential Zen loneliness" (169). In the sort of paradoxical turn that we might expect of haiku aesthetics, sabi is tied in with the idea of compassion, a kind of sensitivity called *aware*. It constitutes a recognition that we're all alone together—not that we're all together really, but that we share our aloneness, or, rather, that our aloneness is something we have in common with all living things. We are all subject to time, united in ephemerality—or, more to the point, all caught alone in the harsh reality of the temporal. But all this is perceived not with grief or despondency but with tranquil acceptance. Sabi is a frustratingly ambiguous concept, such that one expert, Jane Reichhold, has commented, "The Japanese have maintained for centuries that no one can really, truly comprehend what *sabi* really is and thus, they change its definition according to their moods" (10). But the gist of it seems to contain elements of beauty, sadness, tranquillity, and loneliness.

So here we have Thoreau devoting a chapter to the concept of "Solitude," not a far cry at all from aloneness. What is Thoreau's take on the concept? That there is a quality of delight in solitude, certainly, and a greater opportunity to connect with the natural world—look at his satisfaction in enjoying "a delicious evening," and in encountering a whippoorwill, alder leaves, a loon, the pond, a dandelion, the North Star. These observations remind us that the concept of "alone" shares etymological roots with "all one." Thoreau suggests that solitude makes possible a sense of connection to the natural world, reminiscent of Powell's definition of sabi as "the loneliness that allows for appreciation of and communion with nature . . . a way of losing the ego, a way of being in the world unself-consciously" (92). The connections Thoreau makes to the natural world range from small to large, from alder leaves to the Milky Way. The encounters with other humans are described not as connections but as near misses—the scent of a traveller's pipe, a note from a visitor left on a leaf. Or they are unsatisfying—the "musty cheese" that we are at the dinner table.

But it's not quite as simple as saying that real connections are possible only in the nonhuman realm. In the moments of contact with the world outside the self, there are notes of melancholy mixed in with the delight. The hooks with which he fishes are "baited with darkness." And what is he catching with that bait? Pouts. Little fish—but also snits of dissatisfaction. Moments of contact with nature are draughts of "morning air." But they are fleeting moments that "will not keep / quite till noon."

Visitors

three chairs in my house
not much room to utter
the big thoughts in big words

to talk across the pond
to a companion
on the other side

stones thrown into water
breaking each other's
undulations

my withdrawing room
the pine wood
ready for company

the woodchopper
crossing my bean-field early
earning his board

woodcutter
cold woodchuck in his lunch pail
cousin to the pine

satisfied
back to the fire
belly to the table

for the thirsty traveller
lend a dipper
point to the pond

young men
following the beaten path
ceasing to be young

a Sunday walk
railroad men in clean shirts
leaving the village behind

The railroad men strolling to the pond on a Sunday—I think of another of Blyth's thirteen Zen qualities that he says are evident in haiku. Blyth speaks of freedom as a trait of haiku. He defines it, however, not as freedom *to do* something, but as freedom *from something*. Freedom from convention, traditions, and expectations, whether they are societal conventions and traditions (regarding which, see "Economy") or artistic ones. Those railroad men are free from their jobs for a day—but Thoreau also mentions their clean white shirts, which perhaps is part of the celebratory nature of the workers' temporary escape to the woods. Or perhaps the clean shirts serve to remind us of one more set of conventions the men are escaping from, since presumably they are coming to the woods fresh out of church.

Is there a way in which Thoreau does not flout convention? He discounts American dreams of material prosperity, mocks our industriousness, even decries philanthropy. The haiku moments in this chapter demonstrate his unwillingness to keep a home that is designed to accommodate visitors—he entertains in the pines, keeps just three chairs, points the traveller to the pond to get a drink, says that all we need to be happy is a fire behind us and food in front of us. Thoreau is all about critique of the beaten path, even when it's one he made.

The Bean-Field

beans
    impatient to be hoed
        attach me to the earth

                the bean-field
              what right
                    to oust johnswort and the rest

tonight
    my flute has waked echoes
        over the pond

                yellow soil
                    expressing its summer thought
                    in bean leaves and blossoms

my daily work
    making the earth say beans
        instead of grass

woods and pastures and swamps
a rich and various crop
unreaped   .

the hoe in fresh soil
stones from ancient fires
an instant crop

the night-hawk overhead
a mote in the eye
falling from time to time

the hawk
brother of the wave
which he surveys

hen-hawks circling
approaching, leaving
my thoughts

                    plant, hoe, harvest, thresh,
                        sell and taste
                            determined to know beans

    distinctions with the hoe
        level one species
            cultivate another

                        a long war with weeds
                            sun and rain and dews
                                on their side

    at work in the fields
        if only for the tropes
            I give them no manure

                        seeds
                            see if they'll grow in this soil
                                truth and the like

    a grovelling habit
        regarding the soil
            as property

the sun on our fields
          and on the prairies and forests
              without distinction

                                    harvest
                                  seeds for the birds
                                    beans for the woodchucks

I said earlier that few readers would find much of the Blythian ideal of
Zen "non-intellectuality" in Thoreau, and those of us who teach *Walden*
can attest that undergraduates certainly find Thoreau's sentences and
style and vocabulary—in truth, his whole philosophy of life—intellectually challenging enough. And yet I wonder if it is not precisely in
the direction of non-intellectuality that Thoreau is heading. In "The
Bean-Field" he celebrates physical being—being physical—putting
books and human society aside to go work in the field to tend to his
beans.

　　And as I write this, I've just become aware of a possible pun—"being"
sounds like "bean." Is this chapter about Thoreau's work in the "Being
Field"? If so, and if this is an extended pun, what he says about being
is that it works the same way as beans: you've got to prepare the soil for
your being, sow the seeds of being, weed out what is not being, harvest
your being.

　　Puns are another crucial technique in haiku, often serving as pivot
words where levels of meaning branch off. Even in a statement as brief
and apparently straightforward as a haiku, then, we get an indication of
depth and multiplicity beyond the apparently unitary surface impression.
Walden, of course, is peppered with puns. In "Where I Lived, and What

I Lived For," Thoreau speaks of "cultivating" a farmer in conversation, thereby in essence gaining the purchase of a farm, taking the farmer's "word for his deed" — *deed* meaning both action and proof of ownership (81). In "The Bean-Field" there is the wonderful wordplay with the expression "You don't know beans." Actually, Henry shows us, he does know beans, from the ground up.

The wordplay is indicative of another trait of haiku that we might not at first associate with Thoreau, that trait being *karumi*, or "lightness," usually referring to quiet humor and a lightness of language, a simplicity and directness, but also referring to the poet's play with familiar phrasings, giving idioms slight twists that alter meaning or remind us of the actual experiences that underlie idiomatic expressions. Our students may be right in sensing something "heavy" going on in Thoreau, in that he is concerned with serious matters, such as how to live a life, and in that he is highly critical of our cultural mores. And let's face it, Thoreau's prose can be dense because there is so much there intellectually. But much of the serious critique is delivered in very playful language, performing the same functions that wordplay does in haiku — reminding us that no matter how invisible we try to make language as we use it to evoke the natural world, words occasionally explode into double (or multiple) meaning, and that even the plainest language is still language and not the actual world. At the same time, though, the puns often show that everyday language can be traced back to actual experience in nature. As Thoreau puts it in "Walking," he prefers words that still have "earth adhering to their roots" (80).

The Village

village gossip
   the rustle of leaves
      the peeping of frogs

       busy men
         prairie dogs
           each at the mouth of its burrow

a row of men
   sitting on a ladder
      whatever is in the wind

       a dark night
         feet feeling the path
           a hand lifting the latch

in the woods by night
   losing the world
      beginning to find ourselves

                released from jail, shoe mended
                    huckleberries
                        on Fair-Haven Hill

                                the grass
                            when the wind passes over
                                bending

In my introduction I spoke of the emphasis on solitude as a motif in both
nature writing and haiku. Perhaps a chapter dedicated to the goings-on
of "The Village" might be an appropriate place to qualify that claim
somewhat. Recently ecocritics have sought to correct the impression
that nature writing's sole narrative is about the lone male's quest to
discover himself through the agency of remote wilderness — a narrative
template that is typically traced back to Thoreau's influence. See, for
example, David Taylor's lively essay "Giving Up on Language: Or Why
I Quit Reading Thoreau" for a complaint against the overemphasis on
solitude and the quest for "romantic self-discovery" in nature writing,
as exemplified by Thoreau. Or see Ian Marshall and David Taylor's "A
Catskills Dialogue: Looking for John Burroughs, from Wake Robin
to Slabsides," where Taylor recommends Burroughs as a more social
alternative to the solitude motif in nature writing. Of course, plenty of
other nature writers challenge the stereotype as well. For writers like
Terry Tempest Williams and Scott Russell Sanders, for instance, family
connections are central to the encounter with nature, and writers concerned with environmental justice often highlight the social implications
of environmental degradation in natural places nearer to home than
some distant wilderness preserve.

Perhaps his inclusion of a chapter on "The Village" suggests that even Thoreau, despite his misanthropic tendencies, doesn't quite write off the rest of human society in his exploration of the natural world. Similarly, we should recognize that haiku too has a social dimension. Haiku has its origin in the hokku, the opening stanza of a renga, a linked verse form created as a communal enterprise among several poets (it takes a village . . . to write a renga); the most accomplished poet present was usually asked to provide the opening hokku. David Barnhill notes that the opening hokku of a renga functioned as an *aisatsu*, or greeting verse, offered to a host. "That social context," says Barnhill, "is integral to the meaning" (8).

The renga form deserves further explanation, both to illuminate the differences between Japanese and English haiku poetics and to suggest some structural tendencies that seem pertinent to *Walden*. The linked verses of a renga alternate stanzas of 5–7–5 *on* with stanzas of 7–7 *on*. An *on* is a counter of sounds, not really equivalent to a syllable in English; think of it as being akin to a measure of time units—as in the linguistic term *mora*—in quantitative meter. In Japanese a word like the English word *bloom* would constitute three morae—*ba-loo-um*—rather than one syllable. Koji Kawamoto notes that the word *strike* rendered in Japanese becomes five morae: *su-to-ra-i-ku* (293–94). It follows, obviously, that despite the lack of articles in Japanese, seventeen on or morae in Japanese come to less than seventeen syllables in English.[4]

In renga each addition to the series forms a new poem with the section that precedes it. If Poet B adds phrases of 7–7 on after the initial hokku, that makes a discrete poetic entity, a waka of 5–7–5–7–7 on. Poet C then considers B's phrases of 7–7 on and adds another stanza of 5–7–5 on, and the result is another discrete poem of 7–7–5–7–5 on. From there, renga proceeds to a designated number of stanzas (typically thirty-six or one hundred), with formulaic conventions observed along the way. A certain stanza might be required to invoke a particular season, or to be about love, or to provide an image of the moon.

The nature of the links between stanzas was also a key element of the art of renga. It was considered bad form to repeat an image or theme beyond two stanzas. The goal, then, was not at all to construct a coherent narrative line. Far from it—that would be against the rules. This, of course, is very unlike the literary arts we are familiar with in the West, where typically the point is precisely to trace a change in a character and where we think of story as a linear progression from point A to point B. Even when we have a form that is not narrative, like a lyric poem, essentially what we get is the point of epiphany, and the surrounding story is implied. Not so in renga, where if there is any story line, it is simply the ever-changing, saddening, and tranquil beauty of the natural world. There is no protagonist, not even the poet, because there isn't one of those either (since there are several). It adds up to an evocation of life, or life in nature, that refuses to fall into comfortable patterns of individual change or development—the narrative patterns that we find not only in our literature but also in the stories that we make of our own lives here in the West.

You might think of renga as something like pictures at an exhibition, the theme being nature, or the constancy of change—a series of impressions that are truer to reality than a narrative can be, in that they don't add up to a coherent story line, but, rather, show us moments in all their fullness, not as steps along some story line that leads to a point of climax. But no, I take it back, it's not at all like pictures at an exhibition, since each addition is meant to make a complete poem with what immediately precedes. So the "pictures at an exhibition" analogy could hold only if there were just two paintings in each room, brought together in thoughtful juxtaposition. Then the next showroom would have the second of those paintings juxtaposed with another, and so on.

The links between those separate impressions in a renga are based not on chronology or cause and effect; rather, they fall into three categories: first, content links, picking up an image or theme from the previous stanza, often quite subtly, so that an image of a melon, for instance, follows from the roundness of a moon in the previous stanza; second, lexical links, where a word or sound in one stanza is echoed, often in a punning way in the next; and, third, what Bashō called "scent links."

These are tonal or modal qualities, where a visual image in one stanza may be followed up with a totally separate image in the next that evokes the same tone or mood with, perhaps, an aural image. A compass pointing north, say, might be followed by the honking of geese. The same sorts of connections often function within a haiku, providing the subtle link between two different juxtaposed images.

So does any of this have any relevance to *Walden*? Well, there too we do not find a continuous narrative line; rather, there is a series of topics (solitude, visitors, the bean-field, the village, the ponds, and so on) that stand almost separately within the framework of the changing of the seasons. Within each chapter the title suggests another rough framework for a series of impressions and ruminations that circle round that topic. Even within paragraphs, Thoreau's ideas can seem disconnected, with ideas juxtaposed in ways that may take some work to see how they cohere. And from chapter to chapter, too, the links tend to be pretty subtle. Often the connection is one of juxtaposition (just like in a haiku), from "Sounds" to "Solitude," or "Higher Laws" to "Brute Neighbors," or "House-Warming" to "Winter Visitors." Or the observations of sparrows, woodchucks, squirrels, and weeds in "The Bean-Field" lead to the suggested complement of busy men in "The Village." Here Thoreau makes the connection explicit: the gossip he hears in town is "as refreshing in its way as the rustle of leaves and the peeping of frogs. As I walked in the woods to see the birds and squirrels, so I walked to the village to see the men and boys; instead of the wind among the pines I heard the carts rattle" (166).

Walden's chapters often seem arbitrarily joined, but once you start thinking in terms of echoing or juxtaposed content links, lexical links, and scent links, you find some surprising and interesting and meaningful connections. "Economy," from the Greek *oikos*, meaning "house," deals in large part with the building of Thoreau's cabin, which then leads on to the next chapter, "Where I Lived." The rest of the second chapter's title, "And What I Lived For," introduces the book's concern with Thoreau's larger home in the world just beyond his cabin walls. And at this point it is worth remembering that the modern concept of ecology is built on the same *eco* prefix as "Economy." (I am not suggesting that Thoreau is directly invoking the idea of ecology; the term, first used by zoologist Ernst Haeckel, was not coined until 1866, more than a decade after the publication of *Walden*. But given Thoreau's knowledge of Greek, he is certainly punning when he focuses his discussion about how to be "economical" on the reduction of expenses in building a house.) The subtle linking effect continues between chapters two and three as well. The end of "Where I Lived" offers the interesting claim "My instinct tells me that my head is an organ for burrowing" (98), and the next chapter is all about that burrowing we call "Reading." From there we move on to "Sounds" and "the language which all things and events speak without metaphor" (111). And so on.

It can be frustrating to try to read the chapter-to-chapter connections as steps in a progression from here to there, but it is fascinating to try to trace those connections as linkages akin to haiku's ancestral form. The links are there, if we can find them, and they are meaningful, particularly in demonstrating that *Walden* is structured in something other than linear fashion. Overall, of course, the structure is cyclical. But from chapter to chapter, too, the progression is not linear, following a progression within the cycle. Rather, the links are formed by echoes of image, language, and tone.

The Ponds

huckleberries
to know the flavor
ask the partridge

huckleberries
the bloom rubbed off
in the market cart

paddle strike
the surrounding woods filled
with circling sound

in the boat
playing the flute
perch hovering

fishing on a dark night
a tug on the line
interrupting

Walden
clouds and evaporation
inlet and outlet

Walden's water
green and blue
between earth and heaven

waves reflecting the sky
a darker blue
than the sky itself

a row of pitch pines
caught in the pond's rise
the shore shorn

along the shore
smooth rounded white stones
Walled-in Pond

looking into the pond
the depth
of my own nature

the smoothness of the pond
a swallow skims so low
as to touch it

the leap of fishes
the fall of insects
circling dimples

trembling circles seek the shore
every disturbance
smoothed away

the old pond
a mirror no stone can crack
no storm can dim its surface

floating on the pond
as the zephyr wills
the boat touches sand

rich in sunny hours
and summer days
spending lavishly

Walden water
to the village in a pipe
to wash dishes with

a horse
muddying the spring
browsing off the woods onshore

the old pond
not one wrinkle
after all its ripples

no inlet or outlet
a hermit in the woods
the pond's purity

White Pond and Walden
too pure for market value
no muck

Haiku is traditionally viewed as being built out of pure image. Blyth called this tendency "materiality," meaning that haiku focuses on the physical world in concrete language, not on ideas expressed in abstract language, and that it looks at the natural world on its own terms rather than as symbol. But clearly the ponds here are symbolic of something—or of a variety of things. There's something below the surface, which reminds me of Koji Kawamoto's discussion of haiku aesthetics in his study, *The Poetics of Japanese Verse*. Kawamoto says that haiku contain a "base" section—the primary image—and a "superposed" section that serves "to orient the reader to some of the many plausible significances implicated in the base section" (73, 128). That orientation, a "meaning-making hint," often comes in the form of another image that contains a *kigo* word to invoke the seasonal reference, thus suggesting the larger context, symbolic and otherwise, of natural cycles. Sometimes the "meaning-making hint" comes in the form of an allusion or a pun that suggests a second level of meaning. Kawamoto also notes that haiku are typically built around two language registers. First there is *ga*, the elegant, consciously poetic language inherited from the more formal renga tradition, and often serving to invoke that tradition. Ga is typically found in the superposed section. And then there is *zoku*, the plain, simple colloquial language of the base image (66–67).

When I peruse old copies of *Walden*, I am conscious of how much of what is underlined there is of the "meaning-making" variety, ga-like. It is conveyed in the formal diction that our students can find so intimidating, or at least challenging. My discovery in searching for haiku moments in *Walden* is not only that there is an abundance of image and zoku, but also that these base images effectively succeed at incorporating their own meaning making. Thoreau obviously does go to great lengths, especially early in the book, to spell out his ideas in language akin to ga. But as the book proceeds, there seems to be a progressively greater reliance on natural images themselves to carry meaning, with less ga, less disquisition surrounding the images. Yes, there is still likely more abstraction and generalization in the haiku moments that I've extracted from *Walden* than we would expect to find in typical haiku, just as there is more use of personification and metaphor. That is not surprising since Thoreau was making no attempt to exclude such diction and such devices of figurative language in a way that a writer of haiku would. But even when the images and the language of zoku become more and more prominent, Thoreau conveys depth of meaning and resonance—in haiku aesthetics this is called *yūgen*—through language that somehow evokes a further dimension. Which is to say that, like a good transcendentalist (more about this later), he is conscious that, as Emerson says in "Nature," "nature is the symbol of spirit" (17).

Of course, in haiku it's bad form to make the symbolic dimension so apparent that it turns nature into no more than symbol, or primarily symbol, such that the natural image becomes subsumed by its symbolic value. This is the balancing act Thoreau constantly engages in, so that he can see nature as pure symbol one moment, but also wonder in the next, as he does in *A Week*, "Is not Nature, rightly read, that of which she is commonly taken to be the symbol merely?" (382). Tracing the haiku moments in *Walden* gives a good indication of how well— how perfectly—Thoreau balances meaning and symbolism and yūgen with images of nature that are noticed and admired in and of and for themselves.

Baker Farm

cedar trees beyond Flint's Pond
   hoary blue berries
      spiring higher and higher

                  leaping the brook
                    scaring the trout
                      the afternoon before me

afternoon storm
   under a pine
      forked flashes

                  sitting out a storm
                    under that part of the roof
                    which leaks the least

a haste to catch pickerel
   wading in sloughs
      remembering college

the reddening west
rainbow over my shoulder
going fishing

up at dawn
noon finds me by other lakes
at night everywhere at home

sedges and brakes
never to be English hay
the thunder's errand

shelter under a cloud
getting a living
thy sport

household echoes
breathing our own breath
over again

shadows morning and evening
reaching farther
than our daily steps

In Kawamoto's study of haiku aesthetics, he notes that much of the appeal of a haiku—because it is a poem, after all, and not just an expression of a Zen psyche—stems from some "rhetorical anomaly," or distinctiveness in the expression, usually found in the base section (127). The rhetorical anomaly can come in the form of pun, paradox, repetition, hyperbole, something striking in the haiku's sound or its image, or some disruption of syntax or expectation—in short, something in the language, some deviation from language's denotative function, that catches our notice. One flaw evident in much contemporary haiku, it seems to me, is that its emphasis on simplicity and the invisibility of language called "wordless-ness" at times leads to a flatness that often lacks any "rhetorical anomaly," unless the flatness of the language itself is considered the anomaly.

In this regard, too, *Walden* offers a remarkable blend of language that is clear, direct, simple, outward-looking and focused on nature, and at the same time striking in its use of a variety of rhetorical anomalies. The apparent non sequitur in "sedges and brakes / never to be English hay / the thunder's errand" leads us at first to think in terms of cause and effect—are the hedges destined for something other than hay because of the rain?—and then to haiku's more typical pattern of what Gurga calls "effect and effect" (111). The sedges destined for something other than hay and the thunder on its errand are juxtaposed examples of wild things. Note that it's "English" hay that the sedges will never become, the English presumably being the epitome of the civilized, the not wild. The "shadows / reaching farther / than the next step" take on double meaning when we think of the connotative values associated with both "shadows" (suggesting foreboding or gloom) and "steps" (process or progress). Thoreau's language can so readily be converted into effec-tive haiku because beyond being full of interesting images, it exhibits a wonderful array of wordplay, linguistic surprises, various sorts of doubling devices (the puns and paradoxes and word choices that suggest a depth of meaning beyond the surface), and pleasing rhythms often built from balanced sentence structures and an effective use of repetition.

Higher Laws

an impulse to eat woodchuck
   not for my hunger
      but for his wildness

         seeking venison
          loving the wild
            not less than the good

into the forest
   a hunter at first
      then leaving the gun behind

         fishing
          sediment
           sinking to the bottom

a hook of hooks
   angling
      for the pond itself

fishing less and less
a faint intimation
the first streaks of morning

harvest of daily life
the tint of morning
a little star-dust caught

inspired through the palate
berries
eaten on a hillside

jawbone of a hog
sound teeth and tusks
a creature that succeeded

a cool evening
the sound of a flute
stars over far fields

Perhaps a chapter that is entitled "Higher Laws" and that opens with a yearning to devour a woodchuck raw is a good place to discuss the trait of haiku aesthetics that Blyth describes as "non-morality." The reference is to haiku's tendency to avoid judgment and preconception according to any moral code, so that something like a fly settling on dung is as noteworthy as a magnificent sunset—even more so, in fact, since haiku is more likely to focus on the common than the spectacular. Thoreau makes the point that he finds in himself both "an instinct toward a higher, or, as it is named, spiritual life, as do most men, and another toward a primitive rank and savage one." He adds: "I reverence them both . . . the wild not less than the good" (210). Later in the chapter, of course, Thoreau sounds more moralistic, even prudish, in singing the praises of cleanliness, asceticism, and purity. Even then, though, he suggests that the animal part of ourselves, "reptile and sensual," is never far from the surface (219). It is in his acceptance of both the wild and the good, the physical and the spiritual, the particular instance and the higher law, the base and the moral—it is in his juxtaposition of these that the haiku moments of *Walden* often surface.

Brute Neighbors

keeping house
   keeping bright
      the devil's doorknobs

                  water from the spring
                    a loaf of brown bread
                      on the shelf

those clouds
   how they hang
      nothing like it in paintings

                  meditation
                    shall I go to heaven
                    or a-fishing?

whistle
   for my thoughts
      they have left no track

red ants and black ants
　　their Battle of Concord
　　　　fighting for principle

the woods ring
　　the hunter's wild discharge
　　the loon's wild laughter

　　　　the surprise of fishes
　　　　　　a loon amid their schools
　　　　　　　　eighty feet deep

the loon looning
　　a long-drawn unearthly howl
　　　　the woods ring far and wide

　　　　the stillness of the air
　　　　　　the smoothness of the water
　　　　　　　　the loon's long howl

Thoreau asks, "Why do precisely these objects which we behold make a world?" (225). What is *Walden* but a collection of objects beheld—and wondered at? What is the nature of this world? The smoothness of water, the call of a loon, the dive of a loon below the surface, ants in a battle, clouds, a loaf of bread—*Walden* is full of wonder at such things and full of delight in what Blyth called "materiality." It is consistent with the spirit of haiku to behold, as Emerson puts it, "the miraculous in the common" ("Nature" 44). And in gathering these objects for our shared perusal and wonderment, Thoreau also displays the traits of grateful acceptance and love, two more of the Zen qualities Blyth sees as key elements of haiku. Grateful acceptance of and love for all the objects of the world, even when they're not pretty—even amid predation, violence, loss, yearning—even when they seem, at first, nothing particularly remarkable. You hear Thoreau called cranky and curmudgeonly, critical, complaining, and dour, but ultimately *Walden* is a very loving and attentive book. These objects that make up a world—Thoreau reminds us, instance after instance, that they are remarkable.

House-Warming

a-graping
   to the river meadows
      beauty and fragrance and food

              cranberries in meadow grass
                plucked with an ugly rake
                 jammed in Boston

the chestnut woods
   sleeping their long sleep
      under rails

              scarlet maples
                the character of each tree
                reflected in the pond

northeast shore in autumn
   fireside of the pond
      summer's last embers

studying masonry
    to build my chimney
        with second-hand bricks

                        mortaring the chimney
                            our knives thrust into the earth
                                to scour them

the north wind
    cooling the pond
        a fire in the evening

                        rafters with the bark on
                            where flickering shadows
                                may play at evening

a house
    which you have got into
        when you have opened the door

                        sending home
                            each nail
                                a single blow

plastering done
the wind howls
given permission

the wood-pile warming me twice
in the splitting
and on the fire

smoke from my chimney
gives notice to Walden vale
I am awake

Fire and I
keeping house
moles nest in the cellar

a lamp
to lengthen out the day
a sharper blast from the north

looking into it
at evening
always a face in the fire

One of the rhetorical anomalies that catches the attention in Japanese haiku is the use of sound devices—rhyme is avoided, but alliteration and assonance are frequently employed. These are often lost in translation, of course, but in the best contemporary English-language haiku, there is clearly an attention to sound and rhythm. I will not attempt to defend the rhythms of the Thoreauvian haiku I have extracted from *Walden*, since in truth much of the time what I have done is winnow images from longer sentences, thereby losing the original rhythms. In fact, one could make a case that the verbosity of Thoreau's original sentences is a product of his attention to sentence rhythms. (The verbosity is relative, of course; I mean it only in comparison to haiku language.) One of the appeals of Thoreau's prose is the rhythm—but that is one of the contexts out of which I have taken select phrases and images.

But alliteration and assonance remain. I'll offer just one haiku (out of many possible ones) as example here: "sending home / each nail / a single blow." Even in a mere eight words, there is much repetition of sound: the *ing* in *sending* and *single*; the *l* in *nail* and *single*; the *o* in *home* and *blow*. I also note the shift in sound in the repeated *ing*—the first *g* part of a velar nasal, almost silent, the second one hard, the hard one suggesting the arrival, at virtually the same moment, of both the hammer blow and the sunk nail.

Former Inhabitants; and Winter Visitors

evenings by my fireside
snow whirls wildly
without

my path through deep snow
oak leaves lodged in my tracks
melting them deeper

a half-filled cellar hole
a fringe of pines
former inhabitants

apple trees
planted and tended by slaves
their fruit wild and ciderish

a slave's epitaph
the date he died
telling me he had lived

leaping the brook
in hot haste
to get to a fire

the nearness of the fire
our ardor cooled
no frog-pond to throw on it

former inhabitants
a dent in the earth
where hazel and sumacs grow

pitch pine where the chimney stood
sweet-scented black-birch
where the door-stone was

still grows the lilac
door and lintel and sill
a generation gone

a path in deep snow
a dotted line
the same steps coming and going

stepping in my own
deep tracks in snow
filled with heaven's own blue

the limbs of pines
drooping with ice and snow
sharpening their tops

barred owl
launched off the limb of a white pine
feeling his twilight way

wind on my cheek
heathen as I am
I turn the other to it

tracks leading from my door
whittlings on the hearth
the odor of a pipe

visit from a friend
we make amends to Walden
for the long silence

over a dish of gruel
  a bran new
    theory of life

    we sit and whittle
     trying our knives
       admiring the grain of the pine

  fishes in the stream
   coming and going
    clouds float through the western sky

    there too
     expecting the Visitor
      who never comes

Emerson's eulogy for Thoreau singled out for criticism Thoreau's in-
dulgence in paradox, "a habit of antagonism" and "a trick of rhetoric,"
Emerson called it, "of substituting for the obvious word and thought
its diametrical opposite" ("Thoreau" 973). It's a fair charge, I suppose,
highlighting Thoreau's strain of contrariety. It's why Hawthorne once
called Thoreau "the most unmalleable fellow alive—the most tedious,
tiresome, and intolerable—the narrowest and most notional" (117). Thoreau himself makes a point of saying, early on in *Walden*, "The greater

part of what my neighbors call good I believe in my soul to be bad, and if I repent of any thing, it is very likely to be my good behavior. What demon possessed me that I behaved so well?" (10).

In the haiku I have drawn from this chapter, Thoreau's reliance on paradox is evident in several places—an epitaph providing the most lasting indication that someone had actually lived, the leaping of a brook (the essence of coolness) on the way to a fire (in hot haste—tee-hee), new life growing at the scene of an abandoned cabin site, and footprints (sunk into the ground, of course) "filled with heaven's own blue." Even when there's nothing particularly paradoxical in the treatment, Thoreau likes to go by contraries, it seems: snow outside contrasted with fire inside, leaves on snow, even steps "coming and going"—though they are the same steps.

This use of paradox is more than a mere stylistic quirk or pure delight in wordplay, I think, and more than just a reflection of Thoreau's contrary bent. There is something of thematic significance in all this as well. Blyth called the use of paradox in haiku "contradictoriness," and it functions to take us beyond rationality. Where logic may be defied, we can still find truth, but one that we are more likely to grasp with intuition than with reason. Perhaps too the linking of opposites within the space of a haiku or a Thoreauvian sentence—either way, a breath length—is a way of suggesting some sort of ecological connectedness. All these opposites brought together—life/death, snow/leaves, bootprints/heaven, gruel/the life of the mind, coming/going, thought/action—from all this one world is made.

Winter Animals

Walden frozen
 overhung by pines
  bristling with icicles

    a hoot owl
     the frozen earth
      struck with a suitable plectrum

honking of a goose
 the sound of wings
  a tempest in the woods

    screech owl
     responding to the geese
      I too have lungs and a larynx

 whooping of ice in the pond
  restless in bed
   and would fain turn over

squirrels on snow crust
in fits and starts
a leaf blown by the wind

squirrel in a pitch pine
chiding spectators
talking to the universe

squirrel on my wood-pile
thinking of corn
listening to the wind

chickadees
faint flitting lisping notes
icicles in the grass

while I hoe
a sparrow alights
upon my shoulder

in Walden woods a hunter
looking for a lost dog
finding a man

a roadside leaf
a hunter catching it
and playing a wild strain

a single mouse
a whole pine for dinner
its bark gnawed round

light-footed hare
putting the forest
between us

a partridge bursting away
as much expected
as rustling leaves

One of the subtle mysteries of haiku is how something so slight—a breath's worth of image, expressed in language that is marked by simplicity and *karumi*, or "lightness"—can at the same time suggest dimensions of meaning worth meditating upon. How does a haiku manage to be both light and heavy?

Let me offer a couple of examples from "Winter Animals," first "squirrels on snow crust / in fits and starts / a leaf blown by the wind." Karumi is evident in the familiar phrases "fits and starts" and "blown by the wind"—these convey a lightness of language and tone and perhaps a bit of humor as well in the depiction of the busy squirrels seeming constantly distracted by a new project, a new direction in life, every few seconds or so. The *yūgen*, or "depth of meaning," comes in the juxtaposition of the squirrels and the leaves, and our perception that their movements are alike. Lee Gurga points out that the images in a haiku work like spark plugs. Too much distance between the images, such that we don't see how they relate to one another in any meaningful way, and there's no spark. But if the images are too close—again, no spark (40). There has to be just the right degree of separation between the two, enough of a gap for us to read something else between the images—in this case, perhaps a thought that we too, like squirrels and leaves, seem to move through this world in fits and starts, blown about by gusts sending us hither and yon. It's not that the moral lesson as it applies to us humans is primary—it's all of a piece, squirrels, leaves, and us, all subject, as Thoreau might have put it, to the same natural laws.

In "light-footed hare / putting the forest / between us," again there is *karumi* in the play with a familiar idiom (putting something, or space, between us), and *yūgen* in the suggestion that the hare is at home in the forest in a way that self-conscious and civilized humans can perhaps never be. There will always be this gulf between us. Except it's not a gulf, with its suggestion of vast emptiness, but the fullness of forest—to which, sadly, we are never granted complete access, and so it stands between us and the denizens of the wild. In that note of *sabi* and *aware* lie the depths of this, and many another, haiku.

The Pond in Winter

a still winter night
　　some question
　　　　has been put to me

　　　　　　　my morning work
　　　　　　　　I take an axe and pail
　　　　　　　　　　and go in search of water

through a foot of snow
　　then a foot of ice
　　　　window at my feet

　　　　　　　kneeling to drink
　　　　　　　　I look into the parlor
　　　　　　　　　of the fishes

heaven
　　under our feet
　　　　over our heads

                              ah! the pickerel of Walden!
                                Walden all over
                                  Walden all through

with convulsive quirks
   the pickerel give up
      their watery ghosts

                              stories told
                                 of the pond's bottomlessness
                                    they have no foundation

remarkable belief
   the bottomlessness of the pond
      unsounded

                              the pond
                                 deep and pure for a symbol
                                    not an inch can be spared

one known fact
   the bottom of the pond
      the trend of its shores

wearing mittens
a prudent man cutting ice
to cool his summer drink

ice-cutters
unroof the house of fishes
carting off their very air

taking off the only coat
the skin itself
of Walden Pond

the abode of winter
blocks of ice
packed in meadow hay

Walden water
reflecting clouds and trees
evaporating

a solitary loon laughs
a fisherman's reflection
a floating leaf

the servant of Brahma
our buckets grate together
in the same well

"The Pond in Winter" is the chapter I usually choose to show students the transcendental method of deriving spiritual lessons from natural facts. It's the place where Thoreau is most meticulous about gathering data, and where the spiritual as well as physical depths of the pond, the book's central symbol, are plumbed.

But this brings us again to metaphor, central to Thoreau's transcendentalist philosophy and to his style—but generally considered taboo in haiku. Actually, it's not quite accurate to say metaphor is alien to haiku, since of course part of the yūgen of any haiku is likely to arise precisely from its metaphoric implications. And we could also note that, as Lakoff and Johnson have shown us, metaphor is pervasive in language and thought, so if you are using language, no matter how simple and straightforward it appears, undoubtedly metaphor is in there somewhere. It is there even in a word like *straightforward*, for instance, or even in *in*, in a phrase like *in language*, which implies the metaphor of language as container. (Note to structural linguists: I hope you caught the three *in*s in a row in that last line.) But it is also true that haiku typically does all it can to speak, if not absolutely without metaphor, at least without calling attention to it. And that, of course, is not at all true of Thoreau, whose thoughts are built around metaphor—or to put it another way (and in another metaphor), whose thoughts follow paths of metaphor that can be long and meandering.

Rochelle Johnson writes that *Walden* is so "saturated" with metaphor that it "calls more attention to [Thoreau] and his metaphor making than it does to the material world" (191, 200–201). Further, the book's reliance on metaphor at times "leaves readers adrift in philosophizing to such a degree that the real natural world seems far gone," turning the natural world into little more than "a vehicle for the making of allegory, analogy, and symbol" (200–201). Metaphors, says Johnson, are "as likely to partake of culturally-constructed systems of value as they are to convey fresh modes of perception," and so *Walden* becomes complicit in leading us away from an understanding of natural phenomena rather than toward it (199). That's a pretty good summary of all the reasons why haiku tends to avoid metaphor (though the haiku tradition typically avoids presupposing the binary opposition of nature and culture as mutually exclusive entities).

But Johnson also credits Thoreau with a great deal of self-awareness in his use of metaphor, pointing out that he actively grapples with questions about how to write about nature and what role metaphor should play in the process. Johnson traces in Thoreau's writings a change in his descriptive practices, culminating in the uncompleted 750-page Kalendar project, in which, over the course of several years, he recorded on lists and charts the dates of natural phenomena—noting each year just when leaves, blossoms, and fruits appeared, when the ice melted, and when certain birds returned to the region. The shift toward empiricism, says Johnson, began as early as 1850, as Thoreau sought a language that would value nature in and of itself, without the privileging of human affairs that is often implicit in the use of metaphor. Of course, in 1850 Thoreau was still immersed in revisions of *Walden*, which suggests that his concern about the implications of metaphor would be on his mind—and embedded in the text—as he was writing. For all of *Walden*'s immersion in metaphor, we see in it as well a counterbalancing interest in employing a language of pure sensory perception, focused on the natural world itself, sometimes brought in even under the cover of metaphor.

Invariably, my attempts to convert Thoreau's prose into haiku have left in more metaphor than one would typically find in haiku. And at times in these found haiku, I have given the vehicle (the base image) and left out the tenor (the meaning of the image) of Thoreau's metaphors. But the fact that the language of haiku—that is, a language built on deep and detailed sensory perception of the natural world—can be found even amid the densely metaphoric language of much of *Walden* suggests Thoreau's regard for the inherent interest and meaning of the more-than-human world on its own terms and not merely in a human frame of reference. I believe it is also true that one reason we are able to find more and more haiku moments—and haiku images—as *Walden* progresses is that Thoreau more and more allows the images to speak for themselves, without spelling out the metaphoric implications. There are more metaphoric vehicles without attendant tenors (a statement which itself conjures up its own bizarre image). This accompanies what Lawrence Buell has observed about the reduced role of the first person in the book, which Buell says indicates a movement from *ego*centrism to *eco*centrism. Buell points out that the use of the first person drops from 6.6 times per page in the first two chapters to 3.6 in the last five, and references to "Walden," "the pond," and the "wild" increase from 1.8 to 2.3 times per page (122). The shift is related as well, perhaps, to the movement Johnson and others have commented on in the progress of Thoreau's career as a writer—more natural facts, less first-person moralizing about their metaphoric implications. My sense is that the metaphor is still there in Thoreau's later writing, just as it may be implicit in a haiku that apparently dispenses with metaphor. But Thoreau relies ever more fully on the images themselves to carry the freight of suggestion. Each image, then, each observation of the physical world, becomes a koan, the riddly stuff of meditation. The meditation might lead in the direction of metaphor. In haiku, however—and this too is a mark of Thoreau's writing—the original image should never seem all used up by its translation into metaphoric meaning. The image should retain its own aesthetic standing even after its metaphoric potential has been drawn from it.

The standing of the image, the sense that matter matters, is key to Thoreau's transcendentalist practice. And his haiku-like inclinations in this regard are worth exploring. A haiku typically brings together two images and lets them resonate with one another. Neither image is the "real" statement or meaning that is somehow echoed by or explained by the other; both echo one another, and neither is secondary to or attendant upon the other image. Contrast this with Emerson's view, which seems to create a hierarchy of the spiritual and physical worlds, with nature echoing (and yielding primacy to) the spiritual world, the transcendental realm, the ideal world, the real reality that the physical world is the mere echo or shadow of. Thoreau, I think, sets aside this hierarchy and sees resonance between things and ideas, nature and spirit. The hills and valleys don't simply play the part of echo to the human voice's primacy, and they are never overshadowed by their metaphoric meaning, whether or not Thoreau spells out any possible meaning. The sense that the natural world matters perhaps explains why *Walden* seems so chock-full of haiku moments.

Spring

after a cold night
my axe on the ice
resounding

the thundering of the pond
as surely as the buds
expand in spring

bluebird, song sparrow, red-wing
the ice still
a foot thick

the last of the ice
all gone off with the fog
spirited away

a sullen roar the ice   drifting   to the shore

thawing sand
 flowing down a bank
  anticipating the leaf

    the earth
     expressing itself outwardly
      in leaves

the feathers and wings of birds
 the very globe
  winged in its orbit

    the whole tree itself
    but one leaf
     and rivers vaster leaves

thawing clay
 the flow of fingers
  the hand a spreading palm

    the Maker of this earth
    but patented
    a leaf

this is the frost
coming out of the ground
this is Spring

above the fossil earth
a living earth
the leaves of a tree

frost out of its burrow
seeking the sea
migrating to clouds

johnswort, hard-hack, meadow-sweet
the weeds Nature wears
through the winter

red squirrels under my house
deaf to the arguments
of boot heels

the first sparrow!
faint silvery warblings
over bare fields

        marsh-hawk over the meadow
      seeking the first slimy life
        that awakes

                              grass on the hillside
                                the rill out of the ground
                              spring fire

      a grass-blade
        streams from the sod
        into summer

                              song-sparrow's chip-chip
                                from the bushes onshore
                                  helping to crack the ice

      if I could ever find
        the twig—*the twig*—
          the robin sits upon

the honking of geese
unrestrained complaint
mutual consolation

geese spying my light
with hushed clamor wheel
and settle in the pond

circling groping clangor
solitary goose
in the foggy mornings

plants spring and winds blow
to correct the oscillation
of the poles

a single gentle rain
making the grass
many shades greener

the merlin's free
and beautiful fall
the earth lonely beneath it

tenant of the air
its nest in the angle
of a cloud

wildness—where the bittern lurk
and the mink crawls
its belly close to the ground

rambling into
higher and higher grass
on into summer

In "Spring" Thoreau makes the case for living in the present. "We should be blessed if we lived in the present always, and took advantage of every accident that befell us, like the grass which confesses the influence of the slightest dew that falls on it" (314). Thoreau's attempt to capture the presentness of each moment, at the same time framing each moment within the context of seasonal change, is right out of the book of haiku. "Haiku," said Bashō, "is simply what is happening in this place at this moment" (qtd. in Kennedy and Gioia 104). Note that *Walden* gives the impression of being written in the present tense, as if Thoreau is writing it all down as it happens. This is a fiction, of course. Even a scrupulous journal keeper is writing down what happened after the fact. But it's a fiction that has been pervasive in nature writing after Thoreau, such that Scott Slovic has termed it "the written-in-the-field fallacy" (70). But for all its fiction, or even its fallaciousness, it's an attempt to make nature itself fully present, to render the immediacy of contact with nature, as if that contact has happened outside of one's consciousness, filled as it is with the stuff of the past (memory) and the future (planning).

Of course, Thoreau's interest in the present moment, while it may find its fullest flowering in "Spring," is there from the beginning of *Walden*. Way back in "Economy" he writes, "I have been anxious to improve the nick of time, and notch it on my stick too; to stand on the meeting of two eternities, the past and future, which is precisely the present moment; to toe that line" (17). The conception of the present moment as "the meeting of two eternities" conveys some sense of the power of the "haiku moment." The present moment, here, and now, and here, and now, is the one moment where—and when—we are actually in the real world, in direct contact with it, actually perceiving it as opposed to conceptualizing it as memory or expectation. And it is the moment where the vast infinities of past and future meet. This perhaps gives some sense of haiku's fascination with and insistence upon the present moment. And Thoreau's too. To be in the present moment, to be fully in that moment, to be fully awake and aware in that moment—that is what Thoreau aims for, both in his life and in the text of *Walden*. In "Spring," perhaps he arrives at that moment, toeing the line, as he says, between the "two eternities"—not the finish line, but a starting point, the beginning of things, as symbolized by the seasonal reference.

Conclusion

the wild goose
breakfast in Canada
lunch on the Ohio

bison keeping pace
with the seasons
going to greener grass

stone walls around our farms
a universe wider
than our views of it

the West
our own interior
white on the chart

higher latitudes
empty cans piled sky-high
for a sign

a maggot
    loving the soil
        which makes our graves

an unexplored inlet
    the Pacific Ocean
        of one's being alone

a bark from the Gold Coast
    out of sight
        of land

day and night
    sun down, moon down
        and at last earth down too

my path to the pond
    the surface of the earth
        soft and impressible

on the deck of the world
    see the moonlight
        amid the mountains

common sense
the sense of men asleep
expressed by snoring

the blue
of Walden ice
its obscurity

the mists
which envelop the earth
the azure beyond

a man not keeping pace
the music he hears
far away

spring into summer
maturing as soon
as an apple-tree or oak

polishing a walking staff
Kalpa no longer
the pole star

                    the artist of Kouroo
                        the heap of shavings still fresh
                    at his feet

the setting sun
    reflected brightly
        from the windows of the alms-house

                    cultivating sage
                        sell your clothes
                            and keep your thoughts

a spider confined
    to a corner of a garret
        the world large

                    a goose
                        a goose still
                            dress it as you will

a solid bottom everywhere
    the horse sunk in a swamp
        halfway there

driving a nail home
a rivet in the machine
of the universe

knowing a mere
pellicle of the globe
we delve six feet under

joy and sorrow
the burden of a psalm
sung with a nasal twang

water in the river
may flood the parched uplands
this may be the year

an old kitchen table
of apple-tree wood
a bug gnaws its way out

more day to dawn
the sun
but a morning star

Now that I've offered a haiku version of Thoreau's "Conclusion," perhaps it is time for mine. What results from a reading of *Walden* by haiku? How does a discovery of *Walden's* inner haiku contribute to our understanding of Thoreau's accomplishment? What conclusions might be drawn from this literary thought experiment?

The answers might begin with the observation that a great work of literature like *Walden* always seems capable of rewarding a fresh look from a new angle, and that is part of the appeal of a classic. But a reading by haiku seems particularly well suited to the themes of *Walden* and the stylistic bent of Thoreau's writing. I would hope that what is revealed here is a Thoreau who is even more the Poet of the Body as well as the Soul, more entranced with "the *solid* earth! the *actual* world!" (as he exults in "Ktaadn") than we have previously given him credit for—and a little less preoccupied with natural facts that are valued primarily as symbols of spiritual facts (71). Through the lens of haiku, we might see thematic shadings and depths that perhaps we didn't much notice before. We might learn a little more, for instance, about the nature of simplicity, that key theme of Thoreau's, and we might recognize in his discussion of "what he lived for" the aesthetics of wabi, sabi, hosomi, shibumi, or karumi. We might sense that the yūgen of his images, their depths of meaning, might resound in ways that aren't restricted to the human frame of reference. The result is an enriched experience of *Walden* the book—and maybe a set of concepts that might also enrich our experience of Walden the pond, or whatever other particular place in the world suggests depths of meaning for us.

Haiku principles also suggest a resolution to the dilemma that Thoreau kept returning to in his writing career. On the one hand he was tempted to see the world, as Emerson seemed to, as emblematic, valued as metaphor because it was the means of accessing the transcendental realm—and usually leading us from the world around us back to ourselves. And so Thoreau could say, as he does in "Natural History of Massachusetts," "Let us not underrate the value of a fact; it will one day flower in a truth," suggesting that the natural fact is ultimately significant because it leads us to some truth beyond the fact—and presumably the truth is some moral or spiritual truth of special pertinence to humans (23). On the other hand, Thoreau could say, as he does in *A Week on the Concord and Merrimack Rivers*, "Is not Nature, rightly read, that of which she is commonly taken to be the symbol merely?" (382). In these sorts of moments, he seems to believe that nature is itself the transcendental realm — its physicality, its solidity and actuality, is itself the goal of the spiritual quest. Readers of Thoreau often try to sort out exactly where between these two poles Thoreau stands, or where he wants us to stand. The critical consensus these days seems to be that over the course of his career Thoreau become more and more interested in the natural facts in and of and for themselves — so he moved, in essence, from one pole (the transcendental one, where the concern is ultimately for matters of the spirit) to the other (the scientific one, where the concerns are matters of fact).

Haiku, it seems to me, offers a different way of resolving the apparent dilemma, since it might lead us past our insistence on hierarchy (which view of nature does Thoreau *really* value? which is, in his view, superior?) to a place where we can think in terms of juxtaposition as a governing structural principle. It's not one or the other, natural fact or moral meaning, or one above the other — it's eat your cake and still have cake. Neither one is subordinate to or subsumed by the other.

Haiku takes us beyond our predilection for hierarchies of meaning by offering a model for appreciating the natural world simply (a key word there) for itself, in a way that also suggests meaningfulness without resorting to or relying on metaphor as the only means of conveying depths of meaning. As Thoreau in *Walden* comes closer and closer to marrying the two eternities of past and future in the present moment, to a great extent he relinquishes his reliance on metaphor. This pattern he reenacts over the course of his writing career, as evidenced in his journals and the Kalendar project. I am suggesting that physical facts and the present moment lost none of their deep symbolic resonance for Thoreau — and haiku practice demonstrates that the lessening of explanation or metaphor making need not suggest any decrease in the perceived meaningfulness of the natural world. Rather, the resonances rely on suggestion only, with the reader required to fill in the blanks.

Haiku simply make the blanks apparent in the empty space around the words.

I would propose that haiku practice resolves another apparent binary opposition that seems to govern readings of *Walden*—that of self and world. The usual readings posit that in the course of *Walden* Thoreau shifts from self-preoccupation to fascination with the outside world. Indeed, I have suggested as much in tracing the increase in haiku moments in the later chapters of *Walden*. But, again, haiku offers a different way of perceiving things. The point of looking outward is not *erasure* of the self but *absorption*. It's the sensation of being so engaged—or absorbed—in the ah!-inspiring nature of the world that you experience it in some way that is beyond consciousness, or at least beyond self-consciousness. It is not a diminution of self but an expansion of self—an outflow of self to the world that at the same time allows an inflow of world to self. It is a kind of dis-embordering.

In *Wholeness and the Implicate Order* physicist David Bohm maintains that the subject-verb-object structure of our grammar is partially responsible for our experience of the world as divided (from us at least) and fragmented, with subject (us) and object (world) separate—separate and unequal, we might add, with the object world acted upon by the subject self. The grammatical structure of our language leads us to see each thing and concept "as a separate fragment that is essentially fixed and static in its nature" (43). Bohm experiments with a new mode of language less prone to a fragmented view of the world, a mode that he calls the "rheomode," "from the Greek word 'rheo,' to flow" (31). His experiment elevates the status of the verb as a means of restoring wholeness to the world by allowing us to see it as being in constant flow and flux, just as atomic and subatomic particles aren't really fixed and static entities but are themselves in motion, behaving at times more like waves (or quivering strings) than particles. Bohm's point is that "the rheomode does not allow us to discuss the observed fact in terms of separately existent things of an essentially static nature" (46).[5] My point is that haiku—and the haiku-like elements of Thoreau's prose—achieve the same effect.

A haiku presents an act of perception, and its very brevity suggests that the perceived images are anything but static or fixed. In fact, placing an image next to another image almost seems to imply a verb that might clarify how the two images are meant to interact with one another. Placing two images in conjunction is itself a kind of verb, in that it serves to relate one thing to another. We may think of the two images as a kind of still life, but we might also perceive the juxtaposition as a momentary interaction between these two images—and in the next moment we may perceive the energy flowing between two other perceived images.

The flowing effect is furthered by haiku's tendency toward incomplete statement and its preference for present participles, without the helper to complete the verb. The effect is of something fleeting and impermanent. At the same time, if this is not too contradictory, the moments seem removed from time, like the artist of Kouroo and his staff. Those haiku moments that manage to be both ephemeral and eternal, whether they are presented in haiku or found in the text of *Walden*, are moments of perception where the two eternities of past and future meet, flowing together and merging. They are also the brief space where self and world meet, flow together, and merge. There is in fact no hierarchy of self and world here, for there is no fragment of world—a fragment that we might call "self," for instance—that is somehow separate from the world. Nor is there a world separate from self. What I am suggesting, then, is that haiku qualifies as another version of Bohm's rheomode, repairing the fragmentation of our worldview. As it happens, reading *Walden* by haiku reveals the same tendency in Thoreau's worldview, and calls our attention to another theme of the book, another dimension of Thoreau's artistry. *Walden*, too, seeks to restore the wholeness of the world and our experience of it.

Again, though, it's worth recalling the obvious: that Thoreau was clearly not directly influenced by haiku, or even aware of the haiku tradition. How, then, are we to account for the many confluences of theme, style, technique, and aesthetic principles? Is it too far-fetched to speak of a shared worldview between Thoreau at Walden and the world of haiku?

Perhaps "Spring" holds the clue as to the nature of the connection, reminding us that the changing of the seasons is the framework for Thoreau's nature observations—just as it is with haiku. Both haiku and *Walden* feature close attention to the natural world, accompanied by an awareness of the constancy of change, the shift from season to season, the return of each season as the cycle revolves. Constancy and change, the eternal and the ephemeral—this grand and elemental story is told time and again by the smallest details of the natural world. This is the shared fascination of Thoreau and the writer of haiku—and perhaps of all nature writers.

Here is my humble proposition—that paying attention to the details of the natural world leads, perhaps inevitably and perhaps universally, to a state of mind and a literary aesthetic that are marked by these elements: an absorption of self in world and an apparent dissolution of self that might be better understood as an integration of self and world; an attempt to capture that world in some way that deflects attention from the language in which it is being captured, and from the shaper of that language, to the world itself (the aesthetic of "wordlessness," in other words); and a privileging of simplicity and aloneness. In short, all the aesthetic principles we associate with haiku and can find in *Walden*—and in so many other works of nature writing. To offer a few very quick examples: the moment in Faulkner's "The Bear" when Ike leaves behind compass, watch, and gun and can approach the bear and "the wilderness coalesced"; the moment in Elizabeth Bishop's "The Fish" when she lets the fish go in the oil-slicked water and "everything / was rainbow, rainbow, rainbow!"; the "thinking like a mountain" epiphany in Aldo Leopold's *A Sand County Almanac*, when he watches the "fierce green fire" fading in a dying wolf's eyes (Faulkner 30; Bishop 44; Leopold 130). Here is one example of how these too could be rendered into haiku moments:

> we reached the old wolf
>> a fierce green fire
>>> dying in her eyes

The climactic Desolation Peak section of Jack Kerouac's *The Dharma Bums* was in fact built from the haiku in Kerouac's notebooks (one example: " 'Woo!' bird of perfect / balance on the fir / Just moved his tail" [94]). Just about every chapter of Terry Tempest Williams's *Refuge* ends with a moment of pure image that functions, like the haiku in a haibun, to echo thematically or tonally the content of the chapter leading up to it—content that is often emotionally wrenching. One quick illustration, perhaps an apt one for conveying some of the emotional weight and the subject matter of *Refuge*, paralleling as it does the story of the rising waters threatening the Bear River Migratory Bird Refuge with her family's battles with cancer: "the pilgrimage of gulls / from saltwater to fresh / becomes my own" (76).[6] The presence of these haiku-like moments in the American nature-writing tradition is not coincidence—it's a natural outgrowth of shared subject matter.

This is to argue for the pertinence of something akin to a "haiku index" in nature writing—that is, a tabulation of those moments of contact (contact!) with the natural world that are so absorbing that the boundaries of self and world dissolve in a haiku moment. What would be revealed by such an index? First, the high points of a narrative. We might notice, for example, whether the haiku moments occur at the ends of chapters, or if they tend to accumulate, as is the case with *Walden*, with greater frequency toward the end of the narrative. Second, we might calculate through such an index of haiku moments some measure of the writer's tendency to forego ego in favor of an ecocentric absorption in the natural world. I contend that the presence of such moments in a work of nature writing are a distinguishing structural and rhetorical feature of the genre. And at a time when we are hearing calls for ecocriticism to have a clearer sense of its theoretical underpinnings (see Michael Cohen's "Blues in the Green" and Dana Phillips's *The Truth of Ecology*), ecocritics can find in haiku a ready-made set of aesthetic principles that can be fruitfully applied to—or, more to the point, *adapted* to—nature writing.

Of course, it's an open question as to whether the presence of embedded haiku within a work of nature writing serves as any indication of aesthetic excellence. Maybe that depends on the quality of the resulting haiku. It may well be that in the finest works of nature writing we will find, as in the case of *Walden*, the richest blend of simplicity and depth, wabi and yūgen, in the text's found haiku.

PART TWO

Sources and Commentary

Introduction

In each paragraph-length entry below I reproduce the haiku presented in part 1, followed first by the original source passage in *Walden* from which the haiku was extracted, and then by a note offering some quick critical commentary on the phrasing or content of the haiku or the passage it came from. In part 1, I presented the haiku derived from each chapter of *Walden* and then a principle of haiku aesthetics that seemed pertinent to the subject or a theme of that chapter. To some extent I relied on haiku's structural pattern of juxtaposition there, typically allowing (or requiring) readers to find for themselves the connections between the follow-up commentary and the individual haiku. Here, in the notes following each haiku, I make the connections more explicit, showing the specific aesthetic principles applicable to specific haiku. Some of the notes elaborate on points of haiku practice or aesthetics, adding further information and demonstrating with examples. Many of the notes comment on how neatly the images rendered into haiku reinforce or foreground themes of *Walden*. The ability to construct and present images that encapsulate themes is a key element of Thoreau's artistry, one highlighted by the process of discovering haiku moments in the text and isolating them as haiku. In fact, it is precisely that stylistic tendency of Thoreau's that makes possible the finding of haiku moments in the first place.

Though part 2 continues to present information on haiku principles and to suggest their pertinence to themes of *Walden*, the specificity of this section seems particularly useful for demonstrating how Thoreau's prose style seems poetic in specifically haiku-like ways. His is a language of wabi and karumi and shibumi (a preference for familiarity, lightness, astringency), of wordplay, and of an emphasis on simplicity and concreteness of diction. Further, Thoreau's prose is haiku-like in his attention to sound appeal in the way he manipulates rhythm, assonance, and alliteration. The notes often elaborate on the particular rhetorical anomalies inherent in Thoreau's phrasing—whether of word choice, pun, paradox, sound device, or rhythm—that are given featured status by the haiku. Finally, the notes on the found haiku at times call attention to Thoreau's knack for the right word, a word that evokes the actual world and at the same time suggests dimensions of meaning.

Please note that when I praise the phrasing or the image of a haiku, I am not praising my own efforts in shaping the resulting haiku. The credit is intended for haiku master Henry. I think of my efforts here as essentially editorial, selecting from Thoreau's source material in order to foreground its haiku-like tendencies. In that role as editor, on occasion I discuss some of my thinking as I shaped and selected Thoreau's words in order to make them conform to haiku conventions or to make a stronger haiku. Often my comments may serve to highlight principles of haiku style and aesthetics that may be latent or implied in the source passage. My hope here is that readers will learn, or at least further appreciate, two things: first, something about the principles and conventions of haiku as they are applied to particular examples, and second, more about the particular attractions of Thoreau's writing. Selecting bits and pieces of his prose to arrange as haiku certainly heightened my own appreciation for Thoreau's skills not only in demonstrating concepts through images but also in reinforcing his ideas with apt and appealing uses of wordplay and sound devices.

The combination of the haiku with their prose sources in this section owes something to the art of haibun, the blending of highly charged, poetic prose with haiku, as exemplified by works such as Bashō's *The Narrow Road to the Deep North*, or his *Knapsack Notebook*, or Issa's *The Spring of My Life*. Even these classic haibun contain some critical commentary on the art of haiku. Typically, though, in a haibun the haiku usually follows the prose rather than precedes it, and the idea is to echo the tone or theme, or to advance an image that may have appeared in the prose, but not to repeat wording, as these haibun-like entries so clearly do. But I hope that the combination of haiku and source passages here will serve in some ways like traditional haibun, in that they might add new dimensions to the images or the phrasing of the haiku, open up further possibilities, or suggest the sorts of resonances that might emanate from the haiku.

My sense is that rather than reading straight through, readers might best appreciate this section by taking it in bits at a time, dipping into it when you find yourself curious about the aesthetic properties or source passage of a particular haiku, or maybe those from one chapter at a time. As a matter of fact, that's not a bad way to read *Walden* too—sampling here and there as the spirit moves or the season inspires you. Actually, it occurs to me that this "sampling technique" applies to this whole "*Walden* by Haiku" project. I'm referring now to "sampling" as it is done in music (especially in hip-hop or musique concrète), where a songwriter may pick up a musical phrase from a previous song and then feed it back, improvise upon it, or present it in a new context as a way of both offering something new out of familiar materials and commenting on the original. In that sense, this project is sort of a verbal jam session with Henry. Feel free to join in.

Economy

farms, houses, barns, cattle— / easily acquired / hard to get rid of "I see young men, my townsmen, whose misfortune it is to have inherited farms, houses, barns, cattle, and farming tools; for these are more easily acquired than got rid of" (5). This may be a little too moralistic and explanatory for a good haiku, but that's a neat paradox in lines two and three. And this haiku captures Thoreau's wabi sensibility, his sense that material poverty (or simplicity) is a necessary precondition for spiritual richness.

serfs of the soil / digging their graves / as soon as they are born "Who made them serfs of the soil? Why should they eat their sixty acres, when man is condemned to eat only his peck of dirt? Why should they begin digging their graves as soon as they are born?" (5). The cradle–to–grave digging is a metaphor for a life squandered, but Thoreau presents it as pure image, without commentary. This is typical of several of the haiku drawn from this chapter in that it makes a grammatically complete statement. That is not a typical ploy in haiku, where the idea is to resist closure and to give the suggestiveness of the images free reign. Perhaps the tendency toward grammatical completeness in these early haiku reveal their origins in Thoreau's more philosophical and discursive prose from the opening chapter. In later chapters the images come so closely clustered that it seems easier to create juxtapositions of two (or more) images.

compost / the better part of a man / ploughed into the soil "But men labor under a mistake. The better part of the man is soon ploughed into the soil for compost" (5). This offers an example of Thoreau's play with paradox. We might imagine "the better part of a man" to be soul or spirit, but Thoreau suggests that it is the physical being. And that corporeal self comes to the usual humble end of all living things. Our anthropocentrism might consider that an inglorious end, and we can certainly read the passage (and the haiku) that way, with the suggestion that to spend our lives doing nothing but pushing around some soil is a waste of life. On the other hand, Thoreau might consider a human life's contribution to soil nutrients not a bad end result after all. Such ambiguity is encouraged by the open-endedness of a haiku.

the oxen / their vegetable-made bones / the lumbering plough
"One farmer says to me, 'You cannot live on vegetable food solely, for it furnishes nothing to make bones with;' and so he religiously devotes a part of his day to supplying his system with the raw material of bones; walking all the while he talks behind his oxen, which, with vegetable-made bones, jerk him and his lumbering plough along in spite of every obstacle" (9). Blyth says another of the Zen preconditions for haiku is courage—usually meaning the courage to stand up to, and against, social conventions. Is there a pun in the reference to the "lumbering" plough? It, too, in its slow path, has "vegetable-made bones."

ripens my beans / illumines a system of earths / the same sun
"We might try our lives by a thousand simple tests; as, for instance, that the same sun which ripens my beans illumines at once a system of earths like ours. If I had remembered this it would have prevented some mistakes. This was not the light in which I hoed them" (10). Nice juxtaposition here of large (a solar system) and small (beans). Notice that the beans and planets, despite their size differences, echo one another in terms of shape. So does the sun, for that matter. I disrupted the syntax a bit by placing the subject of the actions in the first two lines at the end. This introduces a bit of a rhetorical anomaly and adds an element of surprise. Thus the haiku becomes almost koan-like: what single force could apply to and unify these two very disparate actions—ripening beans and illuminating the solar system?

a seed / rooted firmly in the earth / rising to the heavens "The soil, it appears, is suited to the seed, for it has sent its radicle downward, and it may now send its shoot upward also with confidence. Why has man rooted himself thus firmly in the earth, but that he may rise in the same proportion into the heavens above?" (15). In the haiku version of this, I've left out the metaphoric reference to "man" as the seed in question, but perhaps that metaphoric dimension comes across with the reference to the "heavens," which suggests spiritual as well as botanical yearning.

long ago lost / a hound, a horse, and a dove / I am still on their trail "I long ago lost a hound, a bay horse, and a turtle-dove, and am still on their trail. Many are the travellers I have spoken concerning them, describing their tracks and what calls they answered to. I have met one or two who had heard the hound, and the tramp of the horse, and even seen the dove disappear behind a cloud, and they seemed as anxious to recover them as if they had lost them themselves" (17). This famous passage has inspired Henrik Otterberg's recent book, *Hound, Bay Horse, and Turtle-dove: Obscurity & Authority in Thoreau's Walden,* which collects the many attempts of critics over the years to make some explanatory sense of the intriguing obscurity of the image here. Thoreau's restraint in withholding explanation and letting the image speak for itself suggests the link to haiku.

trying to hear / what is in the wind / I lose my own breath "So many autumn, ay, and winter days, spent outside the town, trying to hear what was in the wind, to hear and carry it express! I well-nigh sunk all my capital in it, and lost my own breath into the bargain, running in the face of it. If it had concerned either of the political parties, depend upon it, it would have appeared in the Gazette with the earliest intelligence" (19). The wind, then, is the gossip in the air around town. Note the language of business and commerce ("capital," "bargain") in some of the phrasing left out of the haiku. Thoreau uses a lot of the language of business in "Economy," of course, but his use of that diction is so clearly metaphoric, I've not included much of that diction in any of the found haiku in this chapter.

the cornice of the palace / finished—the mason / returns to his hut "The mason who finishes the cornice of the palace returns at night perchance to a hut not so good as a wigwam" (34). Thoreau is critiquing our foolishness in going into debt rather than being satisfied with a simpler dwelling. The fifteen pages since the last haiku moment are filled with Thoreau's essay-like pontificating on clothing and shelter.

limestone on my desk / dusted daily / no dust gathers on the grass "I had three pieces of limestone on my desk, but I was terrified to find that they required to be dusted daily, when the furniture of my mind was undusted still, and I threw them out the window in disgust. How, then, could I have a furnished house? I would rather sit in the open air, for no dust gathers on the grass, unless where man has broken ground" (36). I would have loved to include the specificity of *three* pieces of limestone on the desk, but the haiku would have been too wordy. I like the alliteration in "dusted daily," the repetition of sound consonant with the repetition of action.

a borrowed axe / returned / sharper "Near the end of March, 1845, I borrowed an axe and went down to the woods by Walden Pond, nearest to where I intended to build my house, and began to cut down some tall arrowy white pines, still in their youth, for timber. It is difficult to begin without borrowing, but perhaps it is the most generous course thus to permit your fellow-men to have an interest in your enterprise. The owner of the axe, as he released his hold on it, said that it was the apple of his eye; but I returned it sharper than I received it" (40–41). I love the lesson on compassion here, meaning not just helping others, but allowing others to help you—and to receive as well as being able to give with grace. The axe is also an appropriately humble tool for a haiku, which for all its spiritual suggestiveness features a poetics of the ordinary.

a striped snake / lying still in the pond / as long as I stay there "One day, when my axe had come off and I had to cut a green hickory for a wedge, driving it with a stone, and had placed the whole to soak in a pond hole in order to swell the wood, I saw a striped snake run into the water, and he lay on the bottom, apparently without inconvenience, as long as I staid there, or more than a quarter of an hour; perhaps because he had not yet fairly come out of the torpid state. It appeared to me that for a like reason men remain in their present low and primitive condition; but if they should feel the influence of the spring of springs arousing them, they would of necessity rise to a higher and more ethereal life" (41). Here is an example of how, in the early going of *Walden*, Thoreau spells out the moral lesson, the human dimension, that emerges from a natural image. Later, once we have become accustomed to that habit of thought, he may let the image make its suggestions without his spelling them out. The haiku, of course, does not include the little transcendental sermon. There is some humor highlighted by the haiku—while Thoreau is struck by the snake's stillness, he remains equally still, and he does not call attention to his own position.

more friend than foe / cutting the pines / becoming better acquainted While building his cabin: "My days in the woods were not very long ones; yet I usually carried my dinner of bread and butter, and read the newspaper in which it was wrapped, at noon, sitting amid the green pine boughs which I had cut off, and to my bread was imparted some of their fragrance, for my hands were covered with a thick coat of pitch. Before I had done I was more the friend than the foe of the pine tree, though I had cut down some of them, having become better acquainted with it" (42). Thoreau displays again his love of paradox here, along with his compassion (in this case, extended to the trees) and his sense of oneness with the woods.

no curtains / no gazers to shut out / but the sun and the moon "I would observe, by the way, that it costs me nothing for curtains, for I have no gazers to shut out but the sun and moon, and I am willing that they should look in. The moon will not sour milk nor taint meat of mine, nor will the sun injure my furniture or fade my carpet, and if he is sometimes too warm a friend, I find it still better economy to retreat behind some curtain which nature has provided, than to add a single item to the details of housekeeping" (67). More of Thoreau's wabi sensibility—and his grateful acceptance of the frugal conditions of his life.

Where I Lived, and What I Lived For

the landscape retained / its yield carried off / without a wheel-barrow "I found thus that I had been a rich man without any damage to my poverty. But I retained the landscape, and I have since annually carried off what it yielded without a wheelbarrow . . . I have frequently seen a poet withdraw, having enjoyed the most valuable part of a farm, while the crusty farmer supposed that he had got a few wild apples only" (82). The context is that Thoreau is describing his near purchase of a farm. When the deal falls through, he considers himself lucky, for what he harvests from the land requires no plough. Or mortgage.

chanticleer in the morning / standing on his roost / waking the neighbors "I do not propose to write an ode to dejection, but to brag as lustily as chanticleer in the morning, standing on his roost, if only to wake my neighbors up" (84). The "waking the neighbors" line suggests their displeasure, but the first two lines celebrate the proud rooster as a herald of the dawn. The haiku version accentuates the humor, the noble act of heralding a new day serving mainly to annoy the dozing neighbors.

the pond's soft ripples / morning mists / withdrawing to the woods "For the first week, whenever I looked out on the pond it impressed me like a tarn high up on the side of a mountain, its bottom far above the surface of other lakes, and, as the sun arose, I saw it throwing off its nightly clothing of mist, and here and there, by degrees, its soft ripples or its smooth reflecting surface was revealed, while the mists, like ghosts, were stealthily withdrawing in every direction into the woods, as at the breaking up of some nocturnal conventicle" (86). The juxtaposition of images here, the ripples on the pond with the withdrawing mists, suggested the haiku—with, of course, the similes (the mist as ghost or "nightly clothing") omitted.

the wood-thrush heard / from shore to shore / the lake never smoother "This small lake was of most value as a neighbor in the intervals of a gentle rain storm in August, when, both air and water being perfectly still, but the sky overcast, mid-afternoon had all the serenity of evening, and the wood-thrush sang around, and was heard from shore to shore. A lake like this is never smoother than at such a time" (86). As Thoreau gets more focused on the pond and the surrounding woods, and natural images predominate, the haiku moments seem to crop up regularly. The stillness of the scene absorbs even the sound of the wood-thrush.

the earth beyond the pond / a thin crust / floating "It is well to have some water in your neighborhood, to give buoyancy to and float the earth. One value even of the smallest well is, that when you look into it you see that earth is not continent but insular. This is as important as that it keeps butter cool. When I looked across the pond from this peak toward the Sudbury meadows, which in time of flood I distinguished elevated perhaps by a mirage in their seething valley, like a coin in a basin, all the earth beyond the pond appeared like a thin crust insulated and floated even by this small sheet of intervening water, and I was reminded that this on which I dwelt was but *dry land*" (87). Land and water are juxtaposed here, in what Harold Henderson calls haiku's "principle of internal comparison" (18). The description makes the rest of the earth beyond Walden Pond seem like a narrow horizon just past the shores of the pond, like the maps based on a New Yorker's view of America, with everything west of the Hudson amounting to a border along the city's edge.

religious exercise / I get up early / and bathe in the pond "I have been as sincere a worshipper of Aurora as the Greeks. I got up early and bathed in the pond; that was a religious exercise, and one of the best things which I did" (88). "Religious exercise" is a bit abstract for haiku, but I like the pun on "exercise," suggesting both spiritual practice and physical activity. The reference to religion also functions like a more generalized seasonal reference in haiku, which sometimes invoke holidays as seasonal indicators. But instead of identifying a particular holy day, Thoreau observes his sacred rites every day.

a mosquito / touring the cabin at dawn / singing its wrath "Morning brings back the heroic ages. I was as much affected by the faint hum of a mosquito making its invisible and unimaginable tour through my apartment at earliest dawn, when I was sitting with door and windows open, as I could be by any trumpet that ever sang of fame. It was Homer's requiem; itself an Iliad and Odyssey in the air, singing its own wrath and wanderings" (88–89). "I sing," of course, is the standard opening line of an epic. The sense that the smallest things in nature lead lives that matter—on a scale of epic heroes—is the sort of attentiveness to detail we find in haiku. Among haiku masters, Issa is most famous for celebrating the lives and loves and tribulations of the insect world. For Thoreau, the comparisons go the other way as well. If the life of a mosquito can seem epic, human lives can seem inconsequential, as when he says, "Still we live meanly, like ants" (91).

an honest man / counting on his fingers / adding his toes "Our life is frittered away by detail. An honest man has hardly need to count more than his ten fingers, or in extreme cases he may add his ten toes, and lump the rest. Simplicity, simplicity, simplicity!" (91). While haiku typically take nature and the seasons as their subject, this one may be more in the spirit of *senryū*, which generally carry a lighter, more humorous tone and focus more exclusively on human doings and affairs. But we do see in Thoreau's simplicity something akin to the haiku ideals of wabi (the subject matter of simple, familiar, humble things); karumi (usually translated as "lightness"), as in the image of someone adding on his toes to handle numbers eleven through twenty); and hosomi ("slenderness" or "delicacy").

the sleepers / that underlie the rails / sound sleepers, I assure you "We do not ride on the railroad; it rides upon us. Did you ever think what those sleepers are that underlie the railroad? Each one is a man, an Irish-man, or a Yankee-man. The rails are laid on them, and they are covered with sand, and the cars run smoothly over them. They are sound sleepers, I assure you" (92). This might seem like pure metaphor, which is not haiku-like, but it's built on a pun, the sleepers being the wooden ties below the rails. And puns have their place in haiku. In an earlier version, I had the last line read, "each one is a man," which risked making the metaphor too prominent. I trust that the *sound sleepers* phrase still retains the sense that the sleepers refer to men as well as railroad ties.

thrown off the track / a mosquito's wing / on the rails "Let us spend one day as deliberately as Nature, and not be thrown off the track by every nutshell and mosquito's wing that falls on the rails" (97). The first half of that sentence could stand alone as a statement about how and why we might want to lead a haiku life—that is, a life where you notice what's going on in the world around you, by which I mean not political or social concerns, but the call of a new bird and the glint of afternoon sun on pine needles. But we get distracted by minutiae. Maybe we should start noticing the minutiae, especially when they're as interesting as a mosquito's wing.

drinking deeper from the stream / fish in the sky / bottom pebbly with stars "Time is but the stream I go a-fishing in. I drink at it; but while I drink I see the sandy bottom and detect how shallow it is. Its thin current slides away, but eternity remains. I would drink deeper; fish in the sky, whose bottom is pebbly with stars" (98). This is the kind of writing that convinces me that the study of haiku has something to show us about *Walden*. Thoreau simply loves natural images. This is a startlingly beautiful and justly famous one—so clear in its picture, so mysterious and rich and deep in its possible meanings.

Reading

Iliad *on the table / my house to finish / my beans to hoe* "I kept Homer's Iliad on my table through the summer, though I looked at his page only now and then. Incessant labor with my hands, at first, for I had my house to finish and my beans to hoe at the same time, made more study impossible" (99–100). Haiku, they say, is built on nouns. I like how the haiku found here simply lists nouns (*Iliad*, table, house, beans), and yet they manage to convey the message.

reading books of travel / I ask where it was / that I lived "I read one or two shallow books of travel in the intervals of my work, till that employment made me ashamed of myself, and I asked where it was then that *I* lived" (100). The haiku derived from this sentence uncharacteristically uses the past tense, but perhaps that is fitting since it refers to a life, or a portion of a life, that is gone, wasted on pursuits dedicated to something other than living, truly living, in the present.

writing and speech / the firmament with its stars / behind the clouds "However much we may admire the orator's occasional bursts of eloquence, the noblest written words are commonly as far behind or above the fleeting spoken language as the firmament with its stars is behind the clouds" (102). Here is part of Thoreau's genius: his ability to find appropriate natural images to represent abstract concepts like "writing and speech." By the way, note how Thoreau's hierarchy (writing, in its permanence, greater than the transience of speech) reverses the terms of what Jacques Derrida calls phonocentrism, which regards speech as primary and written language as a representation of speech, and thereby necessarily subordinate to speech. Speech is viewed as having presence, says Derrida, and writing the absence of presence. For Thoreau, speech is like the clouds, which come and go, while writing is like the sky, always there, beyond the clouds, or the stars, which are also always there, even when we are blinded by light and cannot perceive them.

there are the stars / and they who can / may read them "There are the stars, and they who can may read them." Verbatim. Thoreau goes on to say, regarding stars, "The astronomers forever comment on and observe them. They are not exhalations like our daily colloquies and vaporous breath" (102). This explains Thoreau's point (above) about writing and speech, but it also speaks (or writes!) beautifully to the miraculous and mysterious nature of the night sky.

books / the oldest and the best / stand on the shelves "Books are the treasured wealth of the world and the fit inheritance of generations and nations. Books, the oldest and the best, stand naturally and rightfully on the shelves of every cottage" (102–3). One of the pleasures of this haiku-extraction project has been the closer attention I have learned to bring to Thoreau's wording. In cutting things down to their essence, I noticed the power of the word choice *stand,* as if there is pride and strength in the posture of the "oldest and best" books on the shelves—the upright books themselves like epic heroes.

man weathercocks / swinging round there / till they are rusty "For my part, I think that they had better metamorphose all such aspiring heroes of universal noveldom into man weathercocks, as they used to put heroes among the constellations, and let them swing round there till they are rusty, and not come down at all to bother honest men with their pranks." Leading up to this, Thoreau has been complaining about "easy reading," featuring such stories as "the nine-thousandth tale about Zebulon and Sephronia, and how they loved as none had ever loved before, and neither did the course of their true love run smooth" (105). The point, I guess, is that those heroes, or those stories, never get anywhere, just going round and round again, like the constellations, or a weather vane. Man weathercocks—what a great and scathing image of lives of quiet desperation. Round and round we go, subject to the whims of every wayfaring wind, never getting anywhere.

the hired man / and Zoroaster / travelling the same road "These same questions that disturb and puzzle and confound us have in their turn occurred to all the wise men . . . The solitary hired man on a farm in the outskirts of Concord, who has had his second birth and peculiar religious experience, and is driven as he believes into silent gravity and exclusiveness by his faith, may think it is not true; but Zoroaster, thousands of years ago, travelled the same road and had the same experience; but he, being wise, knew it to be universal, and treated his neighbors accordingly" (108). Interesting use of the image of the road, especially with the reference to a figure from Eastern philosophy. The way, the path, the road—these are all translations of the Tao, and one follows that path to enlightenment.

Sounds

much published, little printed / the rays which stream / through the shutters "But while we are confined to books, though the most select and classic, and read only particular written languages . . . we are in danger of forgetting the language which all things and events speak without metaphor, which alone is copious and standard. Much is published, but little printed. The rays which stream through the shutter will be no longer remembered when the shutter is wholly removed" (111). Here is another perfectly chosen image to reflect an abstract concept. I read it like this: The world is full of things to notice, as bountiful as sunlight. But only a little bit gets noticed or written about—about as much sunlight as makes it through the shutters. We live our lives with shutters down, and not much of the world gets through. What is a haiku, what is an image, but a bit of attention paid to a piece of sunlight we happen to catch?

a broad margin / from sunrise till noon / my doorway "I love a broad margin to my life. Sometimes, in a summer morning, having taken my accustomed bath, I sat in my sunny doorway from sunrise till noon, rapt in a revery, amidst the pines and hickories and sumachs, in undisturbed solitude and stillness, while the birds sang around or flitted noiseless through the house, until by the sun falling in at my west window, or the noise of some traveller's wagon on the distant highway, I was reminded of the lapse of time" (111). Haiku often has this sense of timelessness, as if all the world and all of time are contained in a single moment, or as if a long stretch of time passes like a single moment. Thoreau here, like the artist of Kouroo in the "Conclusion," has stepped out of time. In the haiku version of the passage, the "broad margin" could refer to either time or space: the whole long luxurious expanse of morning—or the doorway. The description of the dividing line between inside and out as a "broad margin" suggests the amplitude of that space where Thoreau's self encounters the world — reminiscent of the rich habitat of an ecotone, the fertile edge where two ecosystems meet.

a traveller's wagon / the distant highway / corn growing in the night Continuing from the passage above: "I grew in those seasons like corn in the night, and they were far better than any work of the hands would have been. They were not time subtracted from my life, but so much over and above my usual allowance" (111). The interesting juxtaposition of the sound of a distant wagon and corn growing in the night is odd and lovely. Thoreau is like corn growing, I suppose, because that is something one does not notice happening, just as he does not notice the passage of time sitting in his doorway — until the sound of a wagon wakes him from his reverie.

it was morning, and lo, / now it is evening / incessant good fortune "For the most part, I minded not how the hours went. The day advanced as if to light some work of mine; it was morning, and lo, now it is evening, and nothing memorable is accomplished. Instead of singing like the birds, I silently smiled at my incessant good fortune" (112). Grateful acceptance. Joy. Satisfaction. It is difficult to reconcile passages like this with the image of Thoreau as dour curmudgeon.

furniture on the grass / white sand and water / scrubbing the cabin floor "Housework was a pleasant pastime. When my floor was dirty, I rose early, and, setting all my furniture out of doors on the grass, bed and bedstead making but one budget, dashed water on the floor, and sprinkled white sand from the pond on it, and then with a broom scrubbed it clean and white, and by the time the villagers had broken their fast the morning sun had dried my house sufficiently to allow me to move in again, and my meditations were almost uninterrupted" (112–13). There is a tidy paradox here, and a lesson on catharsis, with cleaning accomplished by moving inside things like furniture to the outside, and outside things like water and sand to the inside.

three-legged table / books and pen and ink / standing amid the pines "It was pleasant to see my whole household effects out on the grass, making a little pile like a gypsy's pack, and my three-legged table, from which I did not remove the books and pen and ink, standing amid the pines and hickories. They seemed glad to get out themselves, and as if unwilling to be brought in" (113). The office of a writer, moved out of doors. Which is where and as it should be.

a bird on the next bough / life-everlasting grows / under the table "A bird sits on the next bough, life-everlasting grows under the table, and blackberry vines run round its legs; pine cones, chestnut burs, and strawberry leaves are strewn about. It looked as if this was the way these forms came to be transferred to our furniture, to tables, chairs, and bedsteads, — because they once stood in their midst" (113). The apparent contrast of table and vines, of indoor stuff and out, becomes instead a synthesis, a oneness.

hawks circling / tantivy of wild pigeons / giving voice to the air "As I sit at my window this summer afternoon, hawks are circling about my clearing; the tantivy of wild pigeons, flying by twos and threes athwart my view, or perching restless on the white-pine boughs behind my house, gives a voice to the air; a fishhawk dimples the glassy surface of the pond and brings up a fish; a mink steals out of the marsh before my door and seizes a frog by the shore; the sedge is bending under the weight of the reed-birds flitting hither and thither" (114). One moment, many haiku. I like the conjunction of the visual image (hawks circling) with the aural image (pigeons giving voice to the air). A tantivy, by the way, is a hunting cry (or a full gallop, though that is not the meaning here). If the pigeons can give voice to the air, perhaps Thoreau speaks for the pond and the woods.

rattle of railroad cars / dying and reviving / the beat of a partridge Continuing from above: "For the last half hour I have heard the rattle of railroad cars, now dying away and then reviving like the beat of a partridge, conveying travellers from Boston to the country"

(114). Haiku are nonjudgmental; notice that here the railroad, which at times Thoreau criticizes, fits nicely and naturally into a soundscape that includes ruffed grouses and frogs and reeds along with the rattle of railroad cars.

along the rail line / a track-repairer / the orbit of the earth "The Fitchburg Railroad touches the pond about a hundred rods south of where I dwell. I usually go to the village along its causeway, and am, as it were, related to society by this link. The men on the freight trains, who go over the whole length of the road, bow to me as to an old acquaintance, they pass me so often, and apparently they take me for an employee; and so I am; I too would fain be a track-repairer somewhere in the orbit of the earth" (115). As a writer who points out the many ways our typical lives are flawed, Thoreau is trying to repair the track we are following. Or maybe as a lover and observer of the natural world, he is helping keep the earth on its path, checking the progression of natural cycles.

the locomotive whistle / penetrates my woods / the scream of a hawk "The whistle of the locomotive penetrates my woods summer and winter, sounding like the scream of a hawk sailing over some farmer's yard, informing me that many restless city merchants are arriving within the circle of the town, or adventurous country traders from the other side" (115). In Thoreau's sentence, the comparison of train whistle to hawk's call comes in the form of a simile; in the haiku I juxtaposed the two sounds. The effect is the same, though: to suggest that the train whistle is a piercing but natural sound. And for a hearer who knows how to interpret those sounds, whether raptor or railroad in origin, there is information to be gleaned.

timber on a freight train / the country hands a chair / to the city Still speaking of the locomotive whistle: "Here come your groceries, country; your rations, countrymen! Nor is there any man so independent on his farm that he can say them nay. And here's your pay for them! screams the countryman's whistle; timber like long battering rams going twenty miles an hour against the city's walls, and chairs enough to seat all the weary and heavy laden that dwell within them. With such huge and lumbering civility the country hands a chair to the city" (115–16). This is a little too metaphoric, perhaps, to be typical of haiku, what with the chair representing timber, and the country personified in its passing of the chair. But the way economic geography is reduced to a homey image, that seems fitting for haiku. I would have liked to work in the pun about "lumbering civility," but alas, time is short, and so's a haiku.

freight train / cranberry meadows / raked into the city Continuing from above: "All the Indian huckleberry hills are stripped, all the cranberry meadows are raked into the city" (116). I suppose the phrase *into the city* makes the raking seem more metaphoric than actual, but there is an interesting juxtaposition in the images of a freight train and raking—as if the tracks are like the long tines on a rake.

iron horse / the hills echo / the earth shakes "When I hear the iron horse make the hills echo with his snort like thunder, shaking the earth with his feet, and breathing fire and smoke from his nostrils, (what kind of winged horse or fiery dragon they will put into the new Mythology I don't know,) it seems as if the earth had got a race worthy to inhabit it" (116). Again, the "iron horse" is thoroughly metaphorical, but in its familiarity perhaps it seems less extravagant than the metaphors of train as "winged horse or fiery dragon."

the rising of the sun / clouds stretching to heaven / train going to Boston "I watch the passage of the morning cars with the same feeling that I do the rising of the sun, which is hardly more regular. Their train of clouds stretching far behind and rising higher and higher, going to heaven while the cars are going to Boston, conceals the sun for a minute and casts my distant field into the shade, a celestial train beside which the petty train of cars which hugs the earth is but the barb of the spear" (116–17). I didn't intend the end rhymes of *sun, heaven,* and *Boston,* and perhaps they are subtle enough (with the "un" sounds in *heaven* and

Boston unstressed) to pass for alliteration, which, unlike rhyme, does not egregiously call attention to itself. Those subtle rhymes embedded in Thoreau's sentence, and highlighted by the haiku, show how sensitive Thoreau is to sound as well as rhythm in his prose.

farmer's clocks / set to the train whistle / keeping track of time
"The startings and arrivals of the cars are now the epochs in the village day. They go and come with such regularity and precision, and their whistle can be heard so far, that the farmers set their clocks by them, and thus one well conducted institution regulates a whole country. Have not men improved somewhat in punctuality since the railroad was invented?" (117–18). The pun on *track* may be my insertion (or invention), or perhaps it's a very subtle pun on Thoreau's part; the word *track* appears twice in the rest of the paragraph below what I've quoted here, including the last line ("Keep on your own track, then"). But note that in that line the pun is between *track* as in railroad track and *track* as in a path, rather than a reference to tracking time. But all this discussion suggests how important a word *track* is to Thoreau. He often refers to "tracking" things, as in the lost "hound, bay horse, and turtle-dove" passage. This whole series of railroad images strikes me as particularly haiku-like in its "grateful acceptance" of the railroad, which elsewhere Thoreau condemns. His more usual view of the railroad surfaces at the end of this section, when he complains that a train's approach makes him "get off the track." He concludes the railroad section of "Sounds" by saying, "I will not have my eyes put out and my ears spoiled by its smoke and steam and hissing" (122).

an echo / of the Concord bell / partly the voice of the wood
"Sometimes, on Sundays, I heard the bells, the Lincoln, the Acton, Bedford, or Concord bell, when the wind was favorable, a faint, sweet, and, as it were, natural melody, worth importing into the wilderness. At a sufficient distance over the woods this sound acquires a certain vibratory hum, as if the pine needles in the horizon were the strings of a harp which it swept. All sound heard at the greatest possible distance

produces one and the same effect, a vibration of the universal lyre, just as the intervening atmosphere makes a distant ridge of earth interesting to our eyes by the azure tint it imparts to it. There came to me in this case a melody which the air had strained, and which had conversed with every leaf and needle of the wood, that portion of the sound which the elements had taken up and modulated and echoed from vale to vale. The echo is, to some extent, an original sound, and therein is the magic and charm of it. It is not merely a repetition of what was worth repeating in the bell, but partly the voice of the wood; the same trivial words and notes sung by a wood nymph" (123). This passage and the haiku extracted from it highlight one dimension of Thoreau's theme of awakening—in this case, awakening to the senses. That is also, of course, a recurring haiku theme. Nice juxtaposition of village and wood here, with both audible in the echo. The fact that the town's name is Concord seems apt as well, since village and woods coexist harmoniously—quite literally so—in the sound of the bell.

the evening train gone by / whippoorwills / chant vespers "Regularly at half past seven, in one part of the summer, after the evening train had gone by, the whippoorwills chanted their vespers for half an hour, sitting on a stump by my door, or upon the ridge pole of the house" (123–24). More juxtaposition—the train and the birds, the manufactured and the natural. This one shows how complicated the question of metaphor can be, and demonstrates Emerson's point, in "Nature," that all language, traced back far enough, comes from nature. Vespers means "an evening song" or "an evening worship service," but it comes from the Latin word for evening (vespera), which itself is akin to the Latin word for the evening star (vesper). At first the whippoorwills seem personified as churchgoers, but go back to the root of the word vesper and you find another natural image—so the silence after the evening train has gone by is filled by birdsong and an image of Venus bright on the horizon.

screech owls / their ancient u-lu-lu / oh that I had never been born "When other birds are still the screech owls take up the strain, like mourning women their ancient u-lu-lu. Their dismal scream is truly Ben Jonsonian. Wise midnight hags! It is no honest and blunt tu-whit tu-who of the poets, but, without jesting, a most solemn graveyard ditty . . . Yet I love to hear their wailing, their doleful responses, trilled along the roadside, reminding me sometimes of music and singing birds; as if it were the dark and tearful side of music, the regrets and sighs that would fain be sung . . . They give me a new sense of the variety and capacity of that nature which is our common dwelling. *Oh-o-o-o-o that I never had been bor-r-r-n!* sighs one on this side of the pond, and circles with the restlessness of despair to some new perch on the gray oaks. Then—*that I never had been bor-r-r-n!* echoes another on the farther side with tremulous sincerity, and—*bor-r-r-n!* comes faintly from far in the Lincoln woods" (124–25). Is there justification for my project here? Henry too puts words in someone else's mouth. That is, he renders their utterances in a different form. There is sabi in this passage—a spirit of aloneness that is not less poignant for being shared.

owls / let them do the hooting / for men "I rejoice that there are owls. Let them do the idiotic and maniacal hooting for men" (125). Literary critics speak of the "pathetic fallacy," whereby the natural world seems to share in the mood of a human speaker, as if its very purpose were to serve as an "objective correlative" (to use T. S. Eliot's phrase) for a human state of mind. Or at least that seems to be the role nature typically plays in Western literary aesthetics. But Thoreau seems to be saying something different here, and it seems more in keeping with haiku's sense of connection between the human and the natural, such that neither is subordinated to the other. Even though the owls here speak for us in a sense, they don't take on the coloring of a human protagonist's projected emotional state or lose any of their owlness in the process of expressing something that might not otherwise find expression. Of course Thoreau is being thoroughly lighthearted in saying that owls take care of all the world's idiotic hooting so we don't have to, leaving us free to pursue some other means of expression. But still, the world needs—and we need—the hooting of owls. Thoreau once wrote that "a writer a man writing is the scribe of all nature—he is the corn & the grass & the atmosphere writing" (*Journal* 4:28)—which sounds akin to what David Barnhill says of the haiku tradition, where human expression is seen as being "similar in kind to the tracks of birds" or "akin to birdsong" (10). So too might we say that an owl idiotically hooting is the man and the goose and the morning squall idiotically hooting.

evening / the trump of bullfrogs / trying to sing a catch "Late in the evening I heard the distant rumbling of wagons over bridges,—a sound heard farther than almost any other at night,—the baying of dogs, and sometimes again the lowing of some disconsolate cow in a distant barn-yard. In the mean while all the shore rang with the trump of bullfrogs, the sturdy spirits of ancient wine-bibbers and wassailers, still unrepentant, trying to sing a catch in their Stygian lake" (126). Nice pun on *catch*—a snippet of song as well as an insect dinner. A simple way to teach haiku is to suggest using the three lines to focus on "when," "where," and "what." A typical Thoreauvian paragraph does the same, with the "when" getting particular attention, perhaps because of Thoreau's attention to *Walden's* seasonal framework. Note the complaint about the sounds of wagons (human artifacts) dominating the soundscape rather than blending into the environment of sounds.

frog tr-r-r-oonk / round again and again / that there be no mistake "The most aldermanic, with his chin upon a heart-leaf, which serves for a napkin to his drooling chaps, under this northern shore quaffs a deep draught of the once scorned water, and passes round the cup with the ejaculation *tr-r-r-oonk, tr-r-r-oonk, tr-r-r-oonk!* and straightway comes over the water from some distant cove the same password repeated, where the next in seniority and girth has gulped down to his mark; and when this observance has made the circuit of the shores, then ejaculates the master of ceremonies, with satisfaction, *tr-r-r-oonk!* and each in his turn repeats the same down to the least distended, leakiest, and flabbiest paunched, that there be no mistake; and then the bowl goes round again and again, until the sun disperses the morning mist, and only the patriarch is not under the pond, but vainly bellowing *troonk* from time to time, and pausing for a reply" (126). Funny stuff! Why does this passage make me think of a velvet painting of dogs playing cards? The haiku here is built upon the few bits that do not personify the frogs—though there is also the nice image of the sun dispersing the morning mist.

a winter morning / cockerels crow clear and shrill / the earth resounding "To walk in a winter morning in a wood where these birds abounded, their native woods, and hear the wild cockerels crow on the trees, clear and shrill for miles over the resounding earth, drowning the feebler notes of other birds—think of it! It would put nations on the alert" (127). Again, a clear seasonal reference starts off the sentence—and the haiku. I love the excited expostulation to "think of it!"—as if a cock crowing were such an extraordinary thing. And it is, an ordinary thing that is quite extraordinary, when you think about it, or when you open up your senses and really notice it. I would have liked to get the "think of it!" into the haiku, but there wasn't room. But maybe that's the unspoken dictate of every haiku: "think of it!" That or the hark note of the prefatory stanza in William Carlos Williams's "The Red Wheelbarrow": "so much depends / upon" any apparently commonplace image.

in the Great Snow / no path to the front-yard gate / no gate—no front yard "No cockerels to crow nor hens to cackle in the yard. No yard! but unfenced Nature reaching up to your very sills. A young forest growing up under your windows, and wild sumachs and blackberry vines breaking through into your cellar; sturdy pitch-pines rubbing and creaking against the shingles for want of room, their roots reaching quite under the house . . . Instead of no path to the front-yard gate in the Great Snow,—no gate,—no front yard,—and no path to the civilized world!" (128). The desolate-seeming image (the mood of sabi) in this negative catalog of what is not there around Thoreau's cabin comes at the end of a chapter full of sensory delight. One senses that the lack of civilization's stuff is not to be regarded as emptiness.

Solitude

a delicious evening / the whole body / one sense "This is a delicious evening, when the whole body is one sense, and imbibes delight through every pore" (129). Here is the sense of oneness—the interpenetration of self and world. Thoreau expresses, too, grateful—no, absolutely *delighted*—acceptance of the world, and a claim ("the whole body is one sense"?) that convinces via intuition rather than intellect.

over the water / note of the whippoorwill / borne on the rippling wind "The bullfrogs trump to usher in the night, and the note of the whippoorwill is borne on the rippling wind from over the water" (129). This chapter opens with a flurry of imagistic, haiku-like descriptions, as Thoreau "imbibes delight" in the world around him "through every pore."

fluttering alder leaves / take away my breath / the lake not ruffled Continuing from above: "Sympathy with the fluttering alder and poplar leaves almost takes away my breath; yet, like the lake, my serenity is rippled but not ruffled" (129). Part of the satisfaction of seeking the haiku-like moments and phrases in *Walden* is that it means taking your time through such gorgeous prose and provides the opportunity (or necessity) of savoring such beautiful turns of phrase.

dark now / the wind still roars / the waves still dash "Though it is now dark, the wind still blows and roars in the wood, the waves still dash, and some creatures lull the rest with their notes. The repose is never complete" (129). Here is nature as process. A haiku too is a process, never quite closed off or ended, because its suggestions keep stirring after the words have stopped.

calling cards / a willow wand, a name in pencil / on a yellow leaf "When I return to my house I find that visitors have been there and left their cards, either a bunch of flowers, or a wreath of evergreen, or a name in pencil on a yellow walnut leaf or a chip. They who come rarely to the woods take some little piece of the forest into their hands to play with by the way, which they leave, either intentionally or accidentally. One has peeled a willow wand, woven it into a ring, and dropped it on my table" (129). It is the things of the woods, it seems, that have called to the visitors, just as much as those visitors have called on the hermit-poet of the woods.

a traveller / along the highway / the scent of his pipe "I was frequently notified of the passage of a traveller along the highway sixty rods off by the scent of his pipe" (130). Those who have spent time in the woods claim a certain heightening of the operation of their senses. Haiku practice can have the same effect.

the woods and the pond / the horizon / never quite at our elbows "There is commonly sufficient space about us. Our horizon is never quite at our elbows. The thick wood is not just at our door, nor the pond, but somewhat is always clearing, familiar and worn by us, appropriated and fenced in some way, and reclaimed from Nature. For what reason have I this vast range and circuit, some square miles of unfrequented forest, for my privacy, abandoned to me by men?" (130). In "Walking," Thoreau speaks of the dark days coming when we will not be able to find any unclaimed or open land to walk through. But even today it is easy enough to find woods and fields to walk in, toward a horizon that extends well past our elbows. The expanse of the world is suggested in the open form of the haiku and in the blank space around it.

my own sun and moon and stars / and a little world / all to myself "But for the most part it is as solitary where I live as on the prairies. It is as much Asia or Africa as New England. I have, as it were, my own sun and moon and stars, and a little world all to myself" (130). A beautiful image of aloneness, savored. But notice how vast is the image of solitude—and not the empty or terrifying vastness of a void. Rather, it is a comforting vastness where everything in the universe remains expansive but also seems just close enough without being claustrophobic. The possessive makes "sun and moon and stars" seem comforting, as does the reference to Thoreau's "little" world.

fishing for pouts / baiting the hooks / with darkness "At night there was never a traveller passed my house, or knocked at my door, more than if I were the first or last man; unless it were in the spring, when at long intervals some came from the village to fish for pouts,—they plainly fished much more in the Walden Pond of their own natures, and baited their hooks with darkness,—but they soon retreated, usually with light baskets, and left 'the world to darkness and to me,' and the black kernel of the night was never profaned by any human neighborhood" (130). There's a complex metaphor here, or a series of them: For the fishermen from town, the pond is representative of "their own natures," "baited with darkness," or something dark in their souls. And they're fishing in their own natures for "pouts." Does Thoreau intend the pun? Is a small pout all they can catch in their own natures? I'm not sure what to make of the fact that they leave before the dark of night, leaving that for Henry.

why should I feel lonely? / is not our planet / in the Milky Way? This is verbatim (133), with only the line breaks introduced to suggest the haiku form. The rhetorical questions are not typical for haiku, and the first one does not make an image, but I love the conjunction of small scale (one guy by a pond) and large (the galaxy). The second question is a strange way to answer the first, but its aptness is immediately, if only intuitively, apparent.

I am driftwood in the stream / Indra in the sky / looking down on it "With thinking we may be beside ourselves in a sane sense. By a conscious effort of the mind we can stand aloof from actions and their consequences; and all things, good and bad, go by us like a torrent. We are not wholly involved in Nature. I may be either the driftwood in the stream, or Indra in the sky looking down on it" (135). The play with familiar phrasing here (to be "beside oneself," usually with anger) is akin to Bashō's celebrated karumi, or "lightness." The effect is often to reinvigorate or recast a familiar phrase, as Thoreau does here. To be beside oneself, or to step outside the self through the workings of the intellect, would not seem compatible with the spirit of haiku. And notice that in the process Thoreau becomes personified as Indra (god of the meteorological elements, wind and rain and so on) looking down on the world. But the other self, the one that is not beside the self, the one that is perhaps the original self, becomes driftwood in the stream. This is not personification (nonhuman things seen as human) but its opposite (the human seen as natural object), which suggests an absorption of self in world.

the student at his desk / at work in his field / chopping in his woods "I love to be alone. I never found the companion that was so companionable as solitude. We are for the most part more lonely when we go abroad among men than when we stay in our chambers. A man thinking or working is always alone, let him be where he will. Solitude is not measured by the miles of space that intervene between a man and his fellows. The really diligent student in one of the crowded hives of Cambridge College is as solitary as a dervish in the desert. The farmer can work alone in the field or the woods all day, hoeing or chopping, and not feel lonesome, because he is employed; but when he comes home at night he cannot sit down in a room alone, at the mercy of his thoughts, but must be where he can 'see the folks,' and recreate, and as he thinks remunerate himself for his day's solitude; and hence he wonders how the student can sit alone in the house all night and most of the day without ennui and 'the blues;' but he does not realize that the student, though in the house, is still at work in *his* field, and chopping in *his* woods, as the farmer in his" (135–36). The loneliness that attends us and estranges us when we are not alone, the satisfaction of aloneness when we are—this is sabi.

we meet at meals / a new taste / of that old musty cheese "Society is commonly too cheap. We meet at very short intervals, not having had time to acquire any new value for each other. We meet at meals three times a day, and give each other a new taste of that old musty cheese that we are. We have had to agree on a certain set of rules, called etiquette and politeness, to make this frequent meeting tolerable, and that we need not come to open war" (136). The musty-cheese image in the prose is pure metaphor: we = musty cheese. Many of the haiku I've extracted from *Walden* juxtapose the tenor of the metaphor (the first line here, the "we" part) with the image embedded in the vehicle half of the metaphor (the musty cheese) and leave out the language that indicates the metaphoric dimension (the equals sign, or the "musty cheese *that we are*"). This process works because Thoreau's metaphors give images so complete and interesting that they're capable of standing by themselves.

no more lonely / than the loon in the pond / or the pond itself
"I have a great deal of company in my house; especially in the morning, when nobody calls. Let me suggest a few comparisons, that some one may convey an idea of my situation. I am no more lonely than the loon in the pond that laughs so loud, or than Walden Pond itself" (137). That first sentence presents a wonderful paradox. The images in the third sentence, the origin of the haiku, again strike me as the "reverse personification" technique that Thoreau likes to indulge in. In this case, that reverse personification is a figure of speech called "animalizing," comparing a person to an animal, with Thoreau comparing himself here to a loon. But that term does not quite apply to the self-as-pond image that recurs so often in *Walden*. It suggests again the erasing of boundaries between the self and the world outside the self.

Walden Pond / the blues / in the tint of its waters Continuing from above: "What company has that lonely lake, I pray? And yet it has not the blue devils, but the blue angels in it, in the azure tint of its waters" (137). To build the haiku, I cut out the "devils" and "angels" and then found "azure" unnecessary. I liked isolating "the blues" in the second line, especially after seeing, in the passage about the college student at his desk, that in Thoreau's day "the blues" meant the same thing it does today—despondency. And yet that mood conflicts with the image of beautiful blue water in a pond, which makes for an interesting tension.

dandelion in a pasture / the north star / the south wind "I am no more lonely than a single mullein or dandelion in a pasture, or a bean leaf, or sorrel, or a horse-fly, or a humble-bee. I am no more lonely than the Mill Brook, or a weathercock, or the north star, or the south wind, or an April shower, or a January thaw, or the first spider in a new house" (137). Thoreau expresses such delight in ordinary things in nature. This haiku is one of my favorites, perhaps because of the image of loneliness and strength in the dandelion amid larger forces, and because of the larger visual scale implied by the "north star" and the "south wind."

intelligence with the earth / myself partly leaves / and vegetable mould "Shall I not have intelligence with the earth? Am I not partly leaves and vegetable mould myself?" (138). *Intelligence* does not seem like a haiku word, but I like the elucidation of the term that follows in simple, humble words like *earth*, *leaves*, and *mould*.

a draught of morning air! / it will not keep / quite till noon "For my panacea, instead of one of those quack vials of a mixture dipped from Acheron and the Dead Sea, which come out of those long shallow black-schooner looking wagons which we sometimes see made to carry bottles, let me have a draught of undiluted morning air. Morning air! If men will not drink of this at the fountain-head of the day, why, then, we must even bottle up some and sell it in the shops, for the benefit of those who have lost their subscription ticket to morning time in this world. But remember, it will not keep quite till noon-day even in the coolest cellar, but drive out the stopples long ere that and follow westward the steps of Aurora" (138). Such joy in simple things—a breath of air in the morning. It's not seize the whole day but savor each moment, each breath, and delight in it.

Visitors

three chairs in my house / not much room to utter / the big thoughts in big words "I had three chairs in my house; one for solitude, two for friendship, three for society . . . One inconvenience I sometimes experienced in so small a house, the difficulty of getting to a sufficient distance from my guest when we began to utter the big thoughts in big words. You want room for your thoughts to get into sailing trim and run a course or two before they make their port. The bullet of your thought must have overcome its lateral and ricochet motion and fallen into its last and steady course before it reaches the ear of the hearer, else it may plough out again through the side of the head. Also, our sentences wanted room to unfold and form their columns in the interval. Individuals, like nations, must have suitable broad and natural boundaries, even a considerable neutral ground" (141). The "language as bullet" and "conversation as territorial dispute" comparisons are hilariously hyperbolic, but too overtly metaphoric to serve as the basis of a haiku. I appreciate the wabi-like simplicity of reducing intellectual discourse to the phrase *the big thoughts in big words.*

to talk across the pond / to a companion / on the other side Continuing from above: "I have found it a singular luxury to talk across the pond to a companion on the opposite side" (141). Again, an interesting tension: the natural space separating the two speakers suggests estrangement, but with the possibility of communication still taking place.

stones thrown into water / breaking each other's / undulations Continuing from above: "In my house we were so near that we could not begin to hear,—we could not speak low enough to be heard; as when you throw two stones into calm water so near that they break each other's undulations" (141). The haiku comes from the vehicle half of a metaphor, showing how solidly grounded in the natural world are Thoreau's metaphors.

my withdrawing room / the pine wood / ready for company
"My 'best' room, however, my withdrawing room, always ready for company, on whose carpet the sun rarely fell, was the pine wood behind my house. Thither in summer days, when distinguished guests came, I took them, and a priceless domestic swept the floor and dusted the furniture and kept the things in order" (141–42). Great pun on "drawing room" / "withdrawing room." As in "Economy," Thoreau here plays with the paradox of the outdoors being neat and tidy and clean, swept by the "priceless domestic" nature (or God?)—in contrast to the dirt that accumulates indoors.

the woodchopper / crossing my bean-field early / earning his board "Who should come to my lodge this morning but a true Homeric or Paphlagonian man,—he had so suitable and poetic a name that I am sorry I cannot print it here,—a Canadian, a woodchopper and postmaker, who can hole fifty posts in a day, who made his last supper on a woodchuck which his dog caught . . . He came along early, crossing my bean-field, though without anxiety or haste to get to his work, such as Yankees exhibit. He wasn't a-going to hurt himself. He didn't care if he only earned his board" (145). This admiration for the simplicity and rusticity of Alec Therien's life and ways is the spirit of wabi. Again, notice Thoreau's attention to the setting in time—in this case, his favorite time, early morning. Did he intend the pun on the woodcutter earning "his board"?

woodcutter / cold woodchuck in his lunch pail / cousin to the pine "He was a great consumer of meat, usually carrying his dinner to his work a couple of miles past my house,—for he chopped all summer,—in a tin pail; cold meats, often cold woodchucks, and coffee in a stone bottle which dangled by a string from his belt; and sometimes he offered me a drink . . . In him the animal man chiefly was developed. In physical endurance and contentment he was cousin to the pine and the rock" (145, 146–47). Woodchucks come up a lot in the description of Alec Therien. Elsewhere in the passage Thoreau mentions that Therien would dress and eat the woodchuck that his dog caught. And later the woodcutter is explicitly compared to a woodchuck: "He was so genuine and unsophisticated that no introduction would serve to introduce him, more than if you introduced a woodchuck to your neighbor" (146–47). I suspect more punning on Thoreau's part. I like the oddity of a lunch pail full of cold woodchuck in the second line of the haiku, but I'm not sure that the repetition alone in *woodcutter* and *woodchuck* suggests strongly enough the linking of their identities.

satisfied / back to the fire / belly to the table "One winter day I asked him if he was always satisfied with himself, wishing to suggest a substitute within him for the priest without, and some higher motive for living. 'Satisfied!' said he; 'some men are satisfied with one thing, and some with another. One man, perhaps, if he has got enough, will be satisfied to sit all day with his back to the fire and his belly to the table, by George!' Yet I never, by any manoeuvering, could get him to take the spiritual view of things" (149–50). Ah, the simple life. This harks back, perhaps, to "Economy," where Thoreau speaks of the "vital heat" as the only physiological necessity, and notes that food, shelter, and clothing are simply means of fueling and preserving our vital heat. Where Therien seems content to satisfy only his physiological needs, Thoreau is interested in finding the satisfaction of self-actualization at the top echelon of Abraham Maslow's hierarchy of needs.

for the thirsty traveller / lend a dipper / point to the pond "Many a traveller came out of his way to see me and the inside of my house, and, as an excuse for calling, asked for a glass of water. I told them that I drank at the pond, and pointed thither, offering to lend them a dipper" (130). A whole pond to satisfy a thirst. Ahh!

young men / following the beaten path / ceasing to be young Among his visitors: "Men of business, even farmers, thought only of solitude and employment, and of the great distance at which I dwelt from something or other; and though they said that they loved a ramble in the woods occasionally, it was obvious that they did not. Restless committed men, whose time was all taken up in getting a living or keeping it; ministers who spoke of God as if they enjoyed a monopoly of the subject, who could not hear all kinds of opinions; doctors, lawyers, uneasy housekeepers who pried into my cupboard and bed when I was out,—how came Mrs. —— to know that my sheets were not as clean as hers?—young men who had ceased to be young, and had concluded that it was safest to follow the beaten path of the professions,—all these generally said that it was not possible to do so much good in my position" (153). The reference to the "beaten path" prepares for the image in the "Conclusion" of Thoreau's path to the pond, which is distinct long after he leaves the pond, partly because others have fallen into it, though he would urge all to find their own paths. This ties in with Eastern thought, where the path suggests the path to enlightenment, the way, the truth. These suggestions also echo in Bashō's famous *Oku no Hosomichi*, or, *The Narrow Road to the Deep North*, where the Japanese word for "road" is the same as that for "path" or "way"—and where *Oku*, the remote area of the "Deep North" where Bashō travelled, can also be translated as the "interior."

a Sunday walk / railroad men in clean shirts / leaving the village behind "I had more cheering visitors . . . Children come a-berrying, railroad men taking a Sunday morning walk in clean shirts, fishermen and hunters, poets and philosophers, in short, all honest pilgrims, who came out to the woods for freedom's sake, and really left the village behind" (154). The fact that children head the list of all the "honest pilgrims" here evokes "beginner's mind," that quality of innocence that allows us to see the world fresh at any new moment.

The Bean-Field

beans / impatient to be hoed / attach me to the earth "Meanwhile my beans, the length of whose rows, added together, was seven miles already planted, were impatient to be hoed, for the earliest had grown considerably before the latest were in the ground; indeed they were not easily to be put off. What was the meaning of this so steady and self-respecting, this small Herculean labor, I knew not. I came to love my rows, my beans, though so many more than I wanted. They attached me to the earth, and so I got strength like Antaeus" (154). It is no accident, I think, that the beginnings and endings of *Walden*'s chapters seem such bountiful turf for haiku. That is where Thoreau seeks to ground his discursions, or to bring them back to earth, or to rely on suggestiveness to either prod the reader's mind into activity or set ideas reverberating. The alleged impatience of the beans to be hoed—I thought of that at first as excessive personification, but then it struck me as so transparently a projection of the grower's own impatience that it seemed acceptable in a line that is more about the relationship between Thoreau and his beans than about the beans themselves.

the bean-field / what right / to oust johnswort and the rest "What shall I learn of beans or beans of me? I cherish them, I hoe them, early and late I have an eye to them; and this is my day's work. It is a fine broad leaf to look on. My auxiliaries are the dews and rains which water this dry soil . . . My enemies are worms, cool days, and most of all woodchucks. The last have nibbled for me a quarter of an acre clean. But what right had I to oust johnswort and the rest, and break up their ancient herb garden?" (155). Just as Issa so often expresses sympathy and empathy for insects, so does Thoreau, with his botanical interest, consider the weeds of the garden as well as the lilies of the field.

tonight / my flute has waked echoes / over the pond "When I was four years old, as I well remember, I was brought from Boston to this my native town, through these very woods and this field, to the pond. It is one of the oldest scenes stamped on my memory. And now to-night my flute has waked the echoes over that very water" (156). A nice mingling of beauty, tranquility, and melancholy, very much the spirit, the prevailing mood, of haiku. Rendering the image as haiku sends one more echo across the pond where Bashō's frog long ago jumped.

yellow soil / expressing its summer thought / in bean leaves and blossoms "Removing the weeds, putting fresh soil about the bean stems, and encouraging this weed which I had sown, making the yellow soil express its summer thought in bean leaves and blossoms rather than in worm-wood and piper and millet grass, making the earth say beans instead of grass,—this was my daily work" (155–56). The attribution of "summer thought" to the soil is certainly too indulgent in terms of personification, but I like the image (and the interesting rhetorical anomaly) well enough that I cannot bring myself to weed this one out.

my daily work / making the earth say beans / instead of grass See above for the source. The objection and justification above regarding personification apply here as well. The activity described can be seen as a pleasurably futile pursuit—I mean, you'll never get the earth to talk, and certainly not get it to say what you want it to say. The foolishness of trying to control nature is suggested, but there is also a hint of grateful acceptance for what the earth does give us, even if it is not entirely what we are trying to get from it.

woods and pastures and swamps / a rich and various crop / unreaped "And, by the way, who estimates the value of the crop which Nature yields in the still wilder fields unimproved by man? The crop of *English* hay is carefully weighed, the moisture calculated, the silicates and the potash; but in all the dells and pond holes in the woods and pastures and swamps grows a rich and various crop only unreaped by man" (158). Here is evidence of Thoreau's move beyond anthropocentrism, seeing the value of wild things in something other than human terms.

the hoe in fresh soil / stones from ancient fires / an instant crop
"As I drew a still fresher soil about the rows with my hoe, I disturbed the ashes of unchronicled nations who in primeval years lived under these heavens, and their small implements of war and hunting were brought to the light of this modern day. They lay mingled with other natural stones, some of which bore the marks of having been burned by Indian fires, and some by the sun, and also bits of pottery and glass brought hither by the recent cultivators of the soil. When my hoe tinkled against the stones, that music echoed to the woods and the sky, and was an accompaniment to my labor which yielded an instant and immeasurable crop" (158–59). This "instant crop" is like instant karma reinforcing the compatibility of physical labor with enlightenment. There's a Zen saying that goes something like this: "Before enlightenment, fetch water, gather wood, and rake the garden; after enlightenment, fetch water, gather wood, and rake the garden." Of course, Thoreau finds that the value of hoeing comes not from the hoeing itself but from the arrowheads he finds. Still, he suggests that hoeing provides something of its own reward beyond the harvest that will follow months later.

the night-hawk overhead / a mote in the eye / falling from time to time "The night-hawk circled overhead in the sunny afternoon—for I sometimes made a day of it—like a mote in the eye, or in heaven's eye, falling from time to time with a swoop and a sound as if the heavens were rent, torn at last to very rags and tatters" (159). I like how the haiku isolates the phrase *from time to time*, leaving it reverberating so that it suggests something more than *occasionally*, evoking eons perhaps, as if there were geologic strata layered in the air.

the hawk / brother of the wave / which he surveys "The hawk is aerial brother of the wave which he sails over and surveys, those his perfect air-inflated wings answering to the elemental unfledged pinions of the sea" (159). I wondered about the need for the word *which* in the third line, but I kept it for the images of waves in the repeated *w*'s. The repeated *v* sounds and the long *a*'s in *wave* and *survey* also suggest the connection of hawk and wave. The conception of "brother" hawk introduces personification, but it also creates an intriguing rhetorical anomaly that effectively links the hawk and the wave. In what way is a hawk like a wave? The shape of its wings? Its fluid movement, the surge of a wave between troughs echoed in the soar of a hawk on an updraft? Because the adaptations of a species are always linked to, inseparable from, its habitat?

hen-hawks circling / approaching, leaving / my thoughts "Or sometimes I watched a pair of hen-hawks circling high in the sky, alternately soaring and descending, approaching and leaving one another, as if they were the imbodiment of my own thoughts" (159). I like the ambiguity in the condensed haiku version. Are the hen-hawks approaching and leaving the observer's thoughts, or are they being compared to thoughts in their approaching and leaving?

plant, hoe, harvest, thresh, / sell and taste / determined to know beans "It was a singular experience that long acquaintance which I cultivated with beans, what with planting, and hoeing, and harvesting, and threshing, and picking over, and selling them,—the last was the hardest of all,—I might add eating, for I did taste. I was determined to know beans" (161). Nice pun—Henry didn't cultivate just the beans, he cultivated their acquaintance as well. The wordplay in regard to "he doesn't know beans" I note in the text. Haiku is typically a noun-heavy verse form, which fits with what John Updike described as the "thinginess" of Thoreau's prose, but here's one full of verbs (xxii).

distinctions with the hoe / level one species / cultivate another "Consider the intimate and curious acquaintance one makes with various kinds of weeds,—it will bear some iteration in the account, for there was no little iteration in the labor,—disturbing their delicate organizations so ruthlessly, and making such invidious distinctions with his hoe, levelling whole ranks of one species, and sedulously cultivating another" (161). Here we see more of Thoreau's ecocentrism, as he sees that distinctions made with hoe in hand are based only on perceived usefulness to the human cultivator. The haiku had no room to include the adjective part of *invidious distinctions*, but notice the sound-play in that pairing of words.

a long war with weeds / sun and rain and dews / on their side "That's Roman wormwood,—that's pigweed,—that's sorrel,—that's piper-grass,—have at him, chop him up, turn his roots upward to the sun, don't let him have a fibre in the shade, if you do he'll turn himself t'other side up and be as green as a leek in two days. A long war, not with cranes, but with weeds, those Trojans who had sun and rain and dews on their side. Daily the beans saw me come to their rescue armed with a hoe, and thin the ranks of their enemies, filling up the trenches with weedy dead" (161). With sun and rain and dews on the side of the weeds, the gardener is undermanned. The humor is wry here and at his own expense, as Henry recognizes that his gardening has established an opposition between himself and the elements. This is reminiscent of Woody Allen's lament "I am at two with nature" (reputed to be his first published joke), and of the claim by wilderness philosophers such as Paul Shepard (*Coming Home to the Pleistocene*) that the agricultural revolution was the beginning of human disconnection from the natural world. For the first time, rather than accepting, gratefully, what the earth offered, we sought to make it do our bidding (grow this).

at work in the fields / if only for the tropes / I give them no manure "Those summer days which some of my contemporaries devoted to the fine arts in Boston or Rome, and others to contemplation in India, and others to trade in London or New York, I thus, with the other farmers of New England, devoted to husbandry. Not that I wanted beans to eat, for I am by nature a Pythagorean, so far as beans are concerned [Pythogoras's followers did not eat beans] . . . and exchanged them for rice; but, perchance, as some must work in fields if only for the sake of tropes and expression, to serve a parable-maker one day. It was on the whole a rare amusement, which, continued too long, might have become a dissipation. Though I gave them no manure and did not hoe them all once, I hoed them unusually well as far as I went, and was paid for it in the end, 'there being in truth,' as Evelyn says, 'no compost or laetation whatsoever comparable to this continual motion, repastination, and turning of the mould with the spade'" (162). Here is another case where building the haiku led me to catch a joke. The manure line is separated by a whole sentence from the line about cultivating tropes, and one might take it straight, as if Henry is speaking only of fertilizer for his beans. But he's also talking about the tropes he harvests for parables, and he gives them (or us) "no manure." The joke continues in the quote from Evelyn, who uses the phrase *in truth* in the sense of *in fact* or *verily*. But Thoreau suggests something like this: "in the truth" there is no compost (or manure, for that matter), and in the pursuit of truth there's nothing like working in a bean-field.

seeds / see if they'll grow in this soil / truth and the like "This further experience also I gained. I said to myself, I will not plant beans and corn with so much industry another summer, but such seeds, if the seed is not lost, as sincerity, truth, simplicity, faith, innocence, and the like, and see if they will not grow in this soil, even with less toil and maintenance, and sustain me, for surely it has not been exhausted for these crops" (163–64). Thoreau makes a little dig at his neighbors there, in saying that the soil is not exhausted for crops like truth and faith and innocence; those virtues have evidently not been planted in Concord fields for quite some time. The seeds are clearly metaphoric, but the metaphor follows a great deal of detail about the actual practice of growing beans. Actually, in a sense, the moral message here, about sowing seeds for higher purposes than edibility, is the harvest of Henry's work in the bean-field. Here, in the exhortation, is the fruit of the tropes he has been cultivating. But I like how the phrase *and the like* deflates the idealistic nature of the harvest he seeks.

a grovelling habit / regarding the soil / as property "Ancient poetry and mythology suggest, at least, that husbandry was once a sacred art; but it is pursued with irreverent haste and heedlessness by us, our object being to have large farms and large crops merely . . . By avarice and selfishness, and a grovelling habit, from which none of us is free, of regarding the soil as property, or the means of acquiring property chiefly, the landscape is deformed, husbandry is degraded with us, and the farmer leads the meanest of lives" (165). The haiku taken from this is likely too didactic, but I like its succinctness. Once again, Thoreau's word choice is inspired. To grovel is "to creep with the face to the ground" (so says Webster), where one would literally be "regarding the soil"—that is, looking at it. Of course, to grovel also means "to abase oneself," which is what we do by regarding soil as mere property, thereby losing a sense of farming as "sacred art."

the sun on our fields / and on the prairies and forests / without distinction "We are wont to forget that the sun looks on our cultivated fields and on the prairies and forests without distinction. They all reflect and absorb his rays alike, and the former make but a small part of the glorious picture which he beholds in his daily course" (166). Again, Thoreau takes us beyond anthropocentrism. The sun shines equally bright where it serves our purposes and where it does not. Note that the haiku here runs a little long. While recognizing that English syllables are not the same as Japanese *on* or the quantitative beats called morae (again, that's a linguistic term, not a Japanese word), haiku practitioners in English tend to accept measurement by syllable at least in regard to setting seventeen as the upper limit for a haiku. The truth is that quantitative meter has never really caught on in English, and the nature of our language is such that our words do break down into syllables, stressed and unstressed, so counting by syllables seems to fit our language. The tendency among haiku writers working in English is simply to try to keep each haiku brief, around twelve to fourteen syllables typically, and a few simply transfer haiku's 5–7–5 pattern of Japanese *on* to English syllables (with many, certainly, not even aware of the difference). This haiku, at eighteen syllables, exceeds the customary designated limit, a practice known as *ji-amari* among Japanese haiku poets; Kawamoto calls these extra-long verses "hypermetrical" (247). His point is that generally the number of stresses is not affected, and that is the case here. Counting the beats (the stressed syllables only) instead of all syllables makes this haiku fit the 2–3–2 pattern that Blyth recommends for haiku in English. Perhaps the hyper-metricality here can be justified thematically as well, with the long middle line (eight syllables) suggesting the amplitude of the landscapes described.

harvest / seeds for the birds / beans for the woodchucks "These beans have results which are not harvested by me. Do they not grow for woodchucks partly? The ear of wheat, (in Latin, *spica*, obsoletely *speca*, from *spe*, hope,) should not be the only hope of the husbandman; its kernel or grain (*granum*, from *gerendo*, bearing,) is not all that it bears. How, then, can our harvest fail? Shall I not rejoice also at the abundance of the weeds whose seeds are the granary of the birds?" (166). So the chapter on the bean-field ends with the harvest—not surprising, except that the glad reapers are birds and woodchucks. The chapter begins with focus on the self, a celebration of the beans, according to Henry, because "they attached me to the earth." But at the end his perspective has expanded to recognize how other creatures too participate in the life cycles centered in the garden.

The Village

village gossip / the rustle of leaves / the peeping of frogs "Every day or two I strolled to the village to hear some of the gossip which is incessantly going on there, circulating either from mouth to mouth, or from newspaper to newspaper, and which, taken in homeopathic doses, was really as refreshing in its way as the rustle of leaves and the peeping of frogs" (167). Thoreau here juxtaposes the human and the natural, with an interesting tension. Ordinarily the comparison of human discourse to the peeping of frogs would seem insulting, but this is Thoreau, and he finds nothing invidious in a comparison drawn from the natural world. Only if you are puffed up with a sense of human self-importance will the implied comparison be deemed belittling. Or you could take Thoreau at his word and think of our gossip as something natural and therefore nothing to be ashamed of.

busy men / prairie dogs / each at the mouth of its burrow "In one direction from my house there was a colony of muskrats in the river meadows; under the grove of elms and buttonwoods in the other horizon was a village of busy men, as curious to me as if they had been prairie dogs, each sitting at the mouth of its burrow, or running over to a neighbor's to gossip. I went there frequently to observe their habits" (166). This and the previous passage illustrate the lack of judgment (in the sense of being judgmental) that we typically find in haiku. Everything going on in the world is potentially of interest, and we need not assume that the activities of our own species are the be-all and end-all of significance in the world.

a row of men / sitting on a ladder / whatever is in the wind "I hardly ever failed, when I rambled through the village, to see a row of such worthies, either sitting on a ladder sunning themselves, with their bodies inclined forward and their eyes glancing along the line this way and that, from time to time, with a voluptuous expression, or else leaning against a barn with their hands in their pockets, like caryatides, as if to prop it up. They, being commonly out of doors, heard whatever was in the wind" (168). The haiku highlights the apparently innocent observation that the town's "worthies" are seated "on a ladder" in order to be in position to hear and exchange the latest gossip. But ladders, of course, are intended for vertical use, a means of rising to some higher realm. Ladders and men, one assumes, could be put to some better and higher use. The final line of the haiku — "whatever is in the wind" — can be taken several ways. It could be the subject of the trivial gossip that the ladder loungers hear and exchange, or it could be a note of wonder, along the lines of "What in the world could lead them to waste their time in gossip, when they could be striving toward some higher purpose?" Finally — and this is anachronistic, I know — I hear that *whatever* as uttered, exasperatedly, by a contemporary teen: "Oh, what-*ev*-er."

a dark night / feet feeling the path / a hand lifting the latch "Sometimes, after coming home thus late in a dark and muggy night, when my feet felt the path which my eyes could not see, dreaming and absent-minded all the way, until I was aroused by having to raise my hand to lift the latch, I have not been able to recall a single step of my walk, and I have thought that perhaps my body would find its way home if its master should forsake it, as the hand finds its way to the mouth without assistance" (170). The sense of egolessness here seems fostered by the darkness. In the haiku, I tried to get the sense of "no mind" by focusing on the activities of parts of the body as opposed to the governing consciousness of a whole person. The assonance in the concluding words of the last two lines (*path, latch*) links the two actions, makes them seem of a moment, reflecting the lack of apparent or perceived time that may have passed between the two actions.

in the woods by night / losing the world / beginning to find ourselves "It is a surprising and memorable, as well as valuable experience, to be lost in the woods any time . . . By night, of course, the perplexity is infinitely greater. In our most trivial walks, we are constantly, though unconsciously, steering like pilots by certain well-known beacons and headlands, and if we go beyond our usual course we still carry in our minds the bearing of some neighboring cape; and not till we are completely lost, or turned around, — for a man needs only to be turned round once with his eyes shut in this world to be lost, — do we appreciate the vastness and strangeness of Nature. Every man has to learn the points of compass again as often as he awakes, whether from sleep or any abstraction. Not till we are lost, in other words, not till we have lost the world, do we begin to find ourselves, and realize where we are and the infinite extent of our relations" (170–71). More of Thoreau's penchant for paradox, the sort of self-contradictory truth that convinces by its appeal to intuition rather than to intellect.

released from jail, shoe mended / huckleberries / on Fair-Haven Hill "One afternoon, near the end of the first summer, when I went to the village to get a shoe from the cobbler's, I was seized and put into jail, because, as I have elsewhere related, I did not pay a tax to, or recognize the authority of, the state which buys and sells men, women, and children, like cattle at the door of its senate-house. I had gone down to the woods for other purposes. But, wherever a man goes, men will pursue and paw him with their dirty institutions, and, if they can, constrain him to belong to their desperate odd-fellow society. It is true, I might have run 'amok' against society; but I preferred that society should run 'amok' against me, it being the desperate party. However, I was released the next day, obtained my mended shoe, and returned to the woods in season to get my dinner of huckleberries on Fair-Haven Hill" (171). Note again that the passage opens with a time reference. The night in jail, of course, is the subject of Thoreau's famous and influential "Resistance to Civil Government." I love the way the passage builds to the climax of picking huckleberries: "got thrown in jail, wrote a scathing indictment of American policy and values, prepared the way for Mahatma Gandhi and Martin Luther King Jr. to change history — oh, and here's the really interesting thing: went huckleberry picking on Fair-Haven Hill!"

the grass / when the wind passes over / bending This is actually from Confucius, quoted at the end of "The Village": "'You who govern public affairs, what need have you to employ punishments? Love virtue, and the people will be virtuous. The virtues of a superior man are like the wind; the virtues of a common man are like the grass; the grass, when the wind passes over it, bends'" (172). This follows Thoreau's declaration that he never locked the door of his cabin, and he suggests that robbery would be unknown if everyone lived as simply as he. I changed the verb form from *bends* to *bending* so that it seems more an observation of a particular moment rather than a general truth. Again, Thoreau likes to conclude chapters, as well as open them, with a haiku-like image.

The Ponds

huckleberries / to know the flavor / ask the partridge "The fruits do not yield their true flavor to the purchaser of them, nor to him who raises them for market. There is but one way to obtain it, yet few take that way. If you would know the flavor of huckleberries, ask the cow-boy or the partridge" (173). Lots of Japanese haiku are about the mountain cuckoo, in part, I have to think, because Japanese poets love the sound of the word *hototogisu*. For Thoreau, perhaps "huckleberry" is as key a word.

huckleberries / the bloom rubbed off / in the market cart Continuing from above: "It is a vulgar error to suppose that you have tasted huckleberries who never plucked them. A huckleberry never reaches Boston; they have not been known there since they grew on her three hills. The ambrosial and essential part of the fruit is lost with the bloom which is rubbed off in the market cart, and they become mere provender" (173). It is the firsthand experience, the process, of picking berries, as opposed to the end product purchased at second or third hand, that accounts for the full taste of a huckleberry. It comes from the bush on the hill, the climb of the hill, the sweat on the brow, the gentle tug that urges the bush to release each berry into beckoning fingers. Similarly, those who turn to haiku for their apothegmatic quality or a quick snicker (as in the pseudo-haiku we see about things like computer problems) are not really experiencing the actual world. Picking a berry, writing a haiku, living a worthwhile life: each is a process that involves going to the source and putting in some effort.

paddle strike / the surrounding woods filled / with circling sound "When, as was commonly the case, I had none to commune with, I used to raise the echoes by striking with a paddle on the side of my boat, filling the surrounding woods with circling and dilating sound, stirring them up as the keeper of a menagerie his wild beasts, until I elicited a growl from every wooded vale and hill-side" (174). I like how the repetition of sound (in *surrounding* and *sound*) itself suggests a circling round. In the haiku, I suppose it may not be clear that the paddle is striking the side of the boat, as opposed to the water, but I also like the suggestion that it could be such a quiet day that even a paddle striking water could arouse echoes—and that the aural image of an echo may itself be echoed in the visual image of a whirlpool created by a paddle pulling through water.

in the boat / playing the flute / perch hovering "In warm evenings I frequently sat in the boat playing the flute, and saw the perch, which I seemed to have charmed, hovering around me, and the moon travelling over the ribbed bottom, which was strewed with the wrecks of the forest" (174). Henry, the pied piper of Walden, achieving, once again, oneness.

fishing on a dark night / a tug on the line / interrupting "Sometimes, after staying in a village parlor till the family had all retired, I have returned to the woods, and, partly with a view to the next day's dinner, spent the hours of midnight fishing from a boat by moonlight, serenaded by owls and foxes, and hearing, from time to time, the creaking note of some unknown bird close at hand. These experiences were very memorable and valuable to me,—anchored in forty feet of water, and twenty or thirty rods from the shore, surrounded sometimes by thousands of small perch and shiners, dimpling the surface with their tails in the moonlight, and communicating by a long flaxen line with mysterious nocturnal fishes which had their dwelling forty feet below, or sometimes dragging sixty feet of line about the pond as I drifted in the gentle night breeze, now and then feeling a slight vibration along it, indicative of some life prowling about its extremity, of dull uncertain blundering purpose there, and slow to make up its mind. At length you slowly raise, pulling hand over hand, some horned pout squeaking and squirming to the upper air. It was very queer, especially in dark nights, when your thoughts had wandered to vast and cosmogonal themes in other spheres, to feel this faint jerk, which came to interrupt your dreams and link you to Nature again. It seemed as if I might next cast my line upward into the air, as well as downward into this element which was scarcely more dense. Thus I caught two fishes as it were with one hook" (174–75). That's a long quote, a full paragraph, to offer as source for one haiku of fifteen syllables. But it all seems pertinent. The drifting effect that Thoreau achieves with that long second sentence, a haiku tries to achieve with lots of blank space surrounding very few words. This is one where I hope the coupling of the haiku with the prose from which it is extracted makes the combination read like a haibun (though typically in a haibun the haiku does not directly repeat phrases from the prose that surrounds it or leads to it). The idea of the haiku, of course, is that fishing is primarily a form of meditation, so that the tug on the line may seem an interruption rather than the fulfillment of the fishing excursion's purpose.

Walden / clouds and evaporation / inlet and outlet "The scenery of Walden is on a humble scale, and, though very beautiful, does not approach to grandeur, nor can it much concern one who has not long frequented it or lived by its shore; yet this pond is so remarkable for its depth and purity as to merit a particular description. It is a clear and deep green well, half a mile long and a mile and three quarters in circumference, and contains about sixty-one and a half acres; a perennial spring in the midst of pine and oak woods, without any visible inlet or outlet except by the clouds and evaporation" (175). Here is a lesson on the hydrologic cycle, by haiku.

Walden's water / green and blue / between earth and heaven "Some consider blue 'to be the color of pure water, whether liquid or solid.' But, looking directly down into our waters from a boat, they are seen to be of very different colors. Walden is blue at one time and green at another, even from the same point of view. Lying between the earth and the heavens, it partakes of the color of both" (176). The sound repetition here is highlighted in the haiku: the *w*'s in *Walden* and *water*; the *n*'s in *Walden*, *green*, *between*, and *heaven*; the *r*'s in *water* and *earth*.

waves reflecting the sky / a darker blue / than the sky itself "Like the rest of our waters, when much agitated, in clear weather, so that the surface of the waves may reflect the sky at the right angle, or because there is more light mixed with it, it appears at a little distance of a darker blue than the sky itself; and at such a time, being on its surface, and looking with divided vision, so as to see the reflection, I have discerned a matchless and indescribably light blue, such as watered or changeable silks and sword blades suggest, more cerulean than the sky itself" (177). I have no idea what this means on anything other than the level of the image itself. Are the waves a symbol of art, reflecting reality in a more intense way than reality itself? Does the sky represent ideas, or the realm of spirit being reflected in the ever-changing physical world? Neither Thoreau nor the haiku says, and here's where transcendentalism meets the spirit of haiku—at times the "meaning" of the natural fact can never be pinned down by language. And then we have *yūgen*.

row of pitch pines / caught in the pond's rise / the shore shorn "This rise and fall of Walden at long intervals serves this use at least; the water standing at this great height for a year or more, though it makes it difficult to walk round it, kills the shrubs and trees which have sprung up about its edge since the last rise . . . On the side of the pond next my house, a row of pitch pines fifteen feet high has been killed and tipped over as if by a lever, and thus a stop put to their encroachment; and their size indicates how many years have elapsed since the last rise to this height. By this fluctuation the pond asserts its title to a shore, and thus the *shore* is *shorn*, and the trees cannot hold it by right of possession. These are the lips of the lake on which no beard grows. It licks its chaps from time to time" (181–82). Besides the wordplay and sound-play in "the *shore* is *shorn*," preserved in the haiku, this passage contains two other metaphors omitted from the haiku: the metaphor of the pond claiming legal title or possession of the land, and the personification of the shore as the pond's beardless lips, licking its land-grabbing chops. In this regard, haiku does not always do justice to Thoreau's writing. His prose is wonderfully rich in figurative language, and that is precisely what haiku leaves out in its attempt to present direct apprehension of the thing itself. Thoreau has his haiku moments, for sure, but he explores the linguistic and creative possibilities of all sorts of ways of viewing nature, moving between the poles of anthropocentrism and ecocentrism, just as, in his transcendentalism, he moves between the poles of valuing nature in and of and for itself and valuing nature primarily as symbol. Along these lines, John Updike speaks admiringly of "the athleticism with which [Thoreau] springs from detail to detail, image to image, while still toting something of Transcendentalism's metaphysical burden" (xxii).

along the shore / smooth rounded white stones / Walled-in Pond "Some have been puzzled to tell how the shore became so regularly paved . . . As for the stones, many still think that they are hardly to be accounted for by the action of the waves on these hills; but I observe that the surrounding hills are remarkably full of the same kind of stones, so that they have been obliged to pile them up in walls on both sides of the railroad cut nearest the pond; and, moreover, there are most stones where the shore is most abrupt; so that, unfortunately, it is no longer a mystery to me. I detect the paver. If the name was not derived from that of some English locality,—Saffron Walden, for instance,—one might suppose that it was called, originally, *Walled-in* Pond" (182–83). More wordplay surfaces here in Thoreau's fanciful etymology, which again suggests the hold on him of Emerson's idea that all language, traced back far enough, has its origin in nature.

looking into the pond / the depth / of my own nature "A lake is the landscape's most beautiful and expressive feature. It is earth's eye; looking into which the beholder measures the depth of his own nature. The fluviatile trees next the shore are the slender eye-lashes which fringe it, and the wooded hills and cliffs around are its overhanging brows" (186). I've shifted the haiku from third person to first for greater immediacy. I like the pivoting effect that comes in line three; in line two, the reader thinks the topic is the depth of the pond, only to discover the metaphoric twist in the final line. Of course, we can also read the last line as a possessive claiming of Walden Pond, the essence of the natural world as belonging to Thoreau ("my own nature"). Again, I've left the extensive personification of the pond out of the haiku.

the smoothness of the pond / a swallow skims so low / as to touch it "As you look over the pond westward you are obliged to employ both your hands to defend your eyes against the reflected as well as the true sun, for they are equally bright; and if, between the two, you survey its surface critically, it is literally as smooth as glass, except where the skater insects, at equal intervals scattered over its whole extent, by their motions in the sun produce the finest imaginable sparkle on it, or, perchance, a duck plumes itself, or . . . a swallow skims so low as to touch it" (186–87). I love the sound repetition in *the finest imaginable sparkle*, though the phrase is too long to work into a haiku. But I also like the simplicity and accuracy of the image of the swallow skimming low. Perhaps there is implicit wordplay too in the idea of "swallowing" a gulp of water, and in the skimming "low" suggesting a kind of desecration in daring to disturb the holy water.

the leap of fishes / the fall of insects / circling dimples "From a hill-top you can see a fish leap in almost any part; for not a pickerel or shiner picks an insect from this smooth surface but it manifestly disturbs the equilibrium of the whole lake. It is wonderful with what elaborate-ness this simple fact is advertised,—this piscine murder will out,—and from my distant perch I distinguish the circling undulations when they are half a dozen rods in diameter . . . It is a soothing employment, on one of those fine days in the fall when all the warmth of the sun is fully appreciated, to sit on a stump on such a height as this, overlooking the pond, and study the dimpling circles which are incessantly inscribed on its otherwise invisible surface amid the reflected skies and trees . . .

Not a fish can leap or an insect fall on the pond but it is thus reported in circling dimples, in lines of beauty, as it were the constant welling up of its fountain, the gentle pulsing of its life, the heaving of its breast" (187–88). These lines juxtapose the rise of fishes and fall of insects, both contained within the magic circles of spreading dimples of disturbed water and the shores of the pond itself.

trembling circles seek the shore / every disturbance / smoothed away From the last ellipsis in the previous quote: "Over this great expanse there is no disturbance but it is thus at once gently smoothed away and assuaged, as, when a vase of water is jarred, the trembling circles seek the shore and all is smooth again" (188). The image of the "trembling" ripples widening and dissipating, and the lake becoming smooth once more, evokes the peace of the natural world constantly reasserting, or reestablishing, itself.

the old pond / a mirror no stone can crack / no storm can dim its surface "In such a day, in September or October, Walden is a perfect forest mirror set round with stones as precious to my eye as if fewer or rarer. Nothing so fair, so pure, and at the same time so large, as a lake, perchance, lies on the surface of the earth. Sky water. It needs no fence. Nations come and go without defiling it. It is a mirror which no stone can crack, whose quicksilver will never wear off, whose gilding Nature continually repairs; no storms, no dust, can dim its surface ever fresh;— a mirror in which all impurity presented to it sinks, swept and dusted by the sun's hazy brush,—this the light dust-cloth,—which retains no breath that is breathed on it, but sends its own to float as clouds high above its surface, and be reflected in its bosom still" (188). In this great passage the haiku admittedly still retains the metaphor of pond as mirror, but perhaps this is the place to defend retaining some of Thoreau's metaphoric language even against the typical restraints of haiku: if one of my purposes is to give a synopsis of *Walden*, an abridgment by haiku, well, how could you leave out something this interesting and beautiful about such a central feature of the book's landscape as the pond itself?

And again, paying attention to the details of the language here while in search of haiku constantly pays dividends. In all my readings of *Walden*, this is the first time I've caught the joke about the sun as a *light* dust-cloth. And I even wonder if Thoreau is not invoking the "mirror mirror on the wall" bit from the story of Snow White when he speaks of there being nothing "so fair, so pure" as the pond as mirror. (Who's the fairest of them all? The mirror itself when it's the pond.) Maybe there's another pun when Thoreau says the mirror of Walden "*lies* on the surface of the earth," since all mirrors lie (that is, deal in untruth) in one way or another. Note, of course, that inserting "the old pond" as the opening line invokes Bashō—and suggests that the haiku form itself is a "mirror no stone can crack" and that "no storm can dim its surface."

floating on the pond / as the zephyr wills / the boat touches sand
"I have spent many an hour, when I was younger, floating over its surface as the zephyr willed, having paddled my boat to the middle, and lying on my back across the seats, in a summer forenoon, dreaming awake, until I was aroused by the boat touching the sand, and I arose to see what shore my fates had impelled me to; days whose idleness was the most attractive and productive industry" (191). Does the image of the floating boat oh-so-gently directed by zephyrs convey the luxurious pleasure of so-called idleness without having to spell it out? In a sense, we all live our lives at the whims of wayward zephyrs—and perhaps adopting a spirit of tranquillity might at times be the best course to take.

rich in sunny hours / and summer days / spending lavishly
Continuing from above: "Many a forenoon have I stolen away, preferring to spend thus the most valued part of the day, for I was rich, if not in money, in sunny hours and summer days, and spent them lavishly; nor do I regret that I did not waste more of them in the workshop or the teacher's desk" (191–92). This one suggests another possible defense of allowing in so much metaphor to these Thoreauvian haiku, despite the usual strictures against it in haiku: wordplay is very much in the spirit of haiku, and its purpose is often to alert us to the metaphors implicit in our

conversational language, to make familiar phrases seem fresh and new again. That is the effect of Thoreau's reevaluation of "spending" time wisely. Note too the use of paradox in defining days at work as wasted days, while days on the pond, "stolen" away, help Thoreau accrue a more valuable currency.

Walden water / to the village in a pipe / to wash dishes with "Now the trunks of trees on the bottom, and the old log canoe, and the dark surrounding woods, are gone, and the villagers, who scarcely know where it lies, instead of going to the pond to bathe or drink, are thinking to bring its water, which should be as sacred as the Ganges at least, to the village in a pipe, to wash their dishes with!—to earn their Walden by the turning of a cock or drawing of a plug!" (192). Desecration, thy name is plumbing—though a different sort of plumbing of the pond's depths than Thoreau practices in "The Pond in Winter."

a horse / muddying the spring / browsing off the woods onshore "That devilish Iron Horse, whose ear-rending neigh is heard throughout the town, has muddied the Boiling Spring with his foot, and he it is that has browsed off all the woods on Walden shore; that Trojan horse, with a thousand men in his belly, introduced by mercenary Greeks!" (192). This may be too judgmental regarding the effects of the "Iron Horse," but I like how the lines in the haiku build in length and syllable count, like widening circles, suggesting the expanding ramifications of the railroad. Of course the haiku could be taken literally, the horse considered as a horse rather than a locomotive. But the insinuation would remain that it is implicated in altering its environment for the worse, which would still lead us to consider the horse's browsing as symbolic of our own more drastic acts of "resource extraction."

the old pond / not one wrinkle / after all its ripples "Nevertheless, of all the characters I have known, perhaps Walden wears best, and best preserves its purity. Many men have been likened to it, but few deserve that honor. Though the woodchoppers have laid bare first this shore and then that, and the Irish have built their sties by it, and the railroad has infringed on its border, and the ice-men have skimmed it once, it is itself unchanged, the same water which my youthful eyes fell on; all the change is in me. It has not acquired one permanent wrinkle after all its ripples. It is perennially young, and I may stand and see a swallow dip apparently to pick an insect from its surface as of yore" (192–93). Again, I cannot help but see this passage and haiku as invoking the most famous and most thoroughly analyzed haiku of all, Bashō's "the old pond / a frog jumps / the sound of water." Thinking of Walden as Bashō's old pond makes this passage as resonant as Thoreau's "hound, bay horse, and turtle–dove" parable. The pond retains its purity and remains undamaged and unchanged even after all its far-reaching ripples—far-reaching in terms of both time and geography—and even after the ice-men (critics?) have done their skimming. And every time we find something new in Bashō's old pond, the change is all in us. The echo here, unintended though it be on Thoreau's part, is rich. Bashō's pond poem is said to have changed the art of haiku forever, as he real-ized in this moment of epiphany that haiku should be about simple and familiar things—frogs and ponds—and not extravagant or spectacular ones, like rainbows or roaring rivers or splashy sunsets. Bashō's pond haiku has been extensively commented on, imitated, and evoked—as I have done one more time by arranging Thoreau's comment here in the form of a haiku that echoes once again the sound of water Bashō heard over three hundred years ago. And still—all those wide ripples later—no wrinkles on the pond.

no inlet or outlet / a hermit in the woods / the pond's purity
"I have said that Walden has no visible inlet nor outlet, but it is on the one hand distinctly and indirectly related to Flint's Pond, which is more elevated, by a chain of small ponds coming from that quarter, and on the other directly and manifestly to Concord River, which is lower, by a similar chain of ponds . . . If by living thus reserved and austere, like a hermit in the woods, so long, it has acquired such wonderful purity, who would not regret that the comparatively impure waters of Flint's

Pond should be mingled with it, or itself should ever go to waste its sweetness in the ocean wave?" (194). The effect of juxtaposition in haiku, in this case the hermit and the pond, is to suggest a resonance or an echo effect between the two images, thus achieving the effect of metaphor without directly stating the comparison. It is easy to see here that the hermit partakes of the pond's purity. The full passage, though, makes the isolation of both hermit and pond less complete.

White Pond and Walden / too pure for market value / no muck
"White Pond and Walden are great crystals on the surface of the earth, Lakes of Light. If they were permanently congealed, and small enough to be clutched, they would, perchance, be carried off by slaves, like precious stones, to adorn the heads of emperors; but being liquid, and ample, and secured to us and our successors forever, we disregard them, and run after the diamond of Kohinoor. They are too pure to have a market value; they contain no muck. How much more beautiful than our lives, how much more transparent than our characters, are they!" (199). From the perspective of haiku, that last line of the prose passage, drawing out the moral, is not necessary. The reverberation of the haiku should lead us to consider that moral among the possible resonances of the image in what is preserved as the last line of the haiku, the absence of muck in Walden's water.

Baker Farm

cedar trees beyond Flint's Pond / hoary blue berries / spiring higher and higher "Sometimes I rambled to pine groves, standing like temples, or like fleets at sea, full-rigged, with wavy boughs, and rippling with light, so soft and green and shady that the Druids would have forsaken their oaks to worship in them; or to the cedar wood beyond Flint's Pond, where the trees, covered with hoary blue berries, spiring higher and higher, are fit to stand before Valhalla, and the creeping juniper covers the ground with wreaths full of fruit" (201). This opening sentence of the chapter goes on for half a page, strewn with botanical imagery and extravagant similes. For the haiku, I tried to keep it simple but at the same time attempted to catch some of the excitement of the passage in the last line. I debated whether the situating phrase *beyond Flint's Pond* is necessary, and ultimately decided to keep it, both for the sound repetition (the third "ee" sound in the line along with the internal rhyme of "ond") and for the suggestion that the berries reiterate the color of the pond.

leaping the brook / scaring the trout / the afternoon before me "I set out one afternoon to go a-fishing to Fair-Haven, through the woods, to eke out my scanty fare of vegetables. My way led through Pleasant Meadow, an adjunct of the Baker Farm . . . I thought of living there before I went to Walden. I 'hooked' the apples, leaped the brook, and scared the musquash and the trout. It was one of those afternoons which seem infinitely long before one, in which many events may happen, a large portion of our natural life, though it was already half spent when I started" (203). Again, Thoreau starts by establishing the time frame. On the page before this, there is a description of him standing "in the very abutment of a rainbow's arch" (202); though I did try, that sort of image is a little too glorious for haiku, which specializes in the art of revision—seeing again and anew the stuff of ordinary existence, like a leap over a brook and a free afternoon. To evoke the long afternoon, the blank space around a haiku can speak volumes. I would have loved to get the *musquash* into the middle line, but space would not permit. I opted not to infringe on the blank space around the haiku by making the middle line fuller.

afternoon storm / under a pine / forked flashes Continuing from above: "By the way there came up a shower, which compelled me to stand half an hour under a pine, piling boughs over my head, and wearing my handkerchief for a shed; and when at length I had made one cast over the pickerel-weed, standing up to my middle in water, I found myself suddenly in the shadow of a cloud, and the thunder began to rumble with such emphasis that I could do no more than listen to it. The gods must be proud, thought I, with such forked flashes to rout a poor unarmed fisherman" (203). I've used the old "when, where, what" pattern of haiku here, with the result bringing an unintended juxtaposition: the forks of lightning perhaps evoke the shapes of the pine boughs illuminated by the lightning.

sitting out a storm / under that part of the roof / which leaks the least "So I made haste for shelter to the nearest hut, which stood half a mile from any road, but so much the nearer to the pond, and had long been uninhabited . . . But therein, as I found, dwelt now John Field, an Irishman, and his wife, and several children . . . There we sat together under that part of the roof which leaked the least, while it showered and thundered without" (204). I've inserted a quaint paradox with the idea of sitting *out* a storm by going inside. The repetition of sound in *leaks* and *least* suggests the steady drip.

a haste to catch pickerel / wading in sloughs / remembering college "As I was leaving the Irishman's roof after the rain, bending my steps again to the pond, my haste to catch pickerel, wading in retired meadows, in sloughs and bog-holes, in forlorn and savage places, appeared for an instant trivial to me who had been sent to school and college" (207). The abbreviated version of this in the haiku perhaps alters the meaning somewhat, suggesting a comparison between the sloughs and college, instead of a contrast of environments. But of course the haiku doesn't state either the parallel or the contrast—it can be read both ways—which adds an interesting ambiguity. I would have liked to use *bog-holes* instead of *sloughs* in the middle line, for its more vernacular ring, but that would have made the whole eighteen syllables. The pivot pun on *sloughs* might suggest *slews*—that is, slews of information of the sort you might learn in college.

the reddening west / rainbow over my shoulder / going fishing Continuing from above: "As I ran down the hill toward the reddening west, with the rainbow over my shoulder, and some faint tinkling sounds borne to my ear through the cleansed air, from I know not what quarter, my Good Genius seemed to say,—Go fish and hunt far and wide day by day,—farther and wider,—and rest thee by many brooks and hearth-sides without misgiving" (207). Alternate but ultimately rejected versions of the haiku included the *Good Genius, genius* meaning literally "the attendant spirit of a person or place" (the latter as in *genius loci*). But the *Good Genius* came at the cost of some abstraction and distracted from the color-echoing images of sunset and rainbow.

up at dawn / noon finds me by other lakes / at night everywhere at home The Good Genius, above, still speaking: "Rise free from care before the dawn, and seek adventures. Let the noon find thee by other lakes, and the night overtake thee every where at home" (207). Thoreau recommends joy and grateful acceptance wherever you may find yourself.

sedges and brakes / never to be English hay / the thunder's errand The Good Genius, continuing: "There are no larger fields than these, no worthier games than may here be played. Grow wild according to thy nature, like these sedges and brakes, which will never become English hay. Let the thunder rumble; what if it threaten ruin to farmers' crops? that is not its errand to thee" (207). The haiku follows Thoreau's strange and arresting juxtaposition of images, sedges and thunder, linked by their wildness.

shelter under a cloud / getting a living / thy sport The Good Genius, still: "Take shelter under the cloud, while they [the farmers, above] flee to carts and sheds. Let not to get a living be thy trade, but thy sport. Enjoy the land, but own it not" (207). The idea of shelter under a cloud makes a wonderfully paradoxical image. Isn't the cloud what you might seek shelter from? To get a living—that is, the actual art of discovering how to live, as opposed to having a career and making money, which is how that phrase is usually intended—means to get out (literally) and experience life in a spirit of play, even at the risk of some dampness.

household echoes / breathing our own breath / over again "Men come tamely home at night only from the next field or street, where their household echoes haunt, and their life pines because it breathes its own breath over again; their shadows morning and evening reach farther than their daily steps. We should come home from far, from adventures, and perils, and discoveries every day, with new experience and character" (208). The haiku highlights the assonance here (the *o*'s in *household, echoes, own,* and *over*), and of course *breathing our own breath* itself is a kind of echo. The claustrophobic interior here contrasts with the celebratory description of the previous one, where more comfortable shelter is found under a cloud.

shadows morning and evening / reaching farther / than our daily steps (See above.) I considered inserting a "next" step in place of "daily" steps. The idea of shadows reaching farther than daily steps suggests constrained circumstances, with the addressee not stretching legs and life far enough to escape his own shadows (or fears). But the idea of shadows reaching farther than the "next" step suggests trepidation about the future, the sort of thing that renders us, in life, immobile. While I might have chosen "next" step, I try to keep Thoreau's wording intact as much as possible, as long as it is consistent with haiku principles and form. I also admire the added dimension of saying these are "morning and evening" shadows. My choice might have been to suggest only evening shadows, with the length of the shadows suggesting that the action, or inaction, takes place late in the day. But that would have been a bad choice—the inclusion of morning as well as evening shadows suggests a sense of foreboding that stretches farther than the possibilities of one's existence even before that first step is taken. It all makes for a very bleak haiku.

Higher Laws

an impulse to eat woodchuck / not for my hunger / but for his wildness "As I came home through the woods with my string of fish, trailing my pole, it being now quite dark, I caught a glimpse of a wood-chuck stealing across my path, and felt a strange thrill of savage delight, and was strongly tempted to seize and devour him raw; not that I was hungry then, except for that wildness which he represented" (210). This is the opening sentence of the chapter, and again Thoreau begins with a startling image—all the more startling to read of such "savage delight" after a chapter heading promising the headier stuff of ethics and philosophy. Again, temporal framing prepares for the image, as in haiku.

seeking venison / loving the wild / not less than the good Continuing from above: "Once or twice, however, while I lived at the pond, I found myself ranging the woods, like a half-starved hound, with a strange abandonment, seeking some kind of venison which I might devour, and no morsel could have been too savage for me. The wildest scenes had become unaccountably familiar. I found in myself, and still find, an instinct toward a higher, or, as it is named, spiritual life, as do most men, and another toward a primitive rank and savage one, and I reverence them both. I love the wild not less than the good" (210). As with the previous haiku, the second two lines may be a little heavy on commentary and short on image, but both contain paradox or juxtaposition, making for an interesting rhetorical anomaly.

into the forest / a hunter at first / then leaving the gun behind "We cannot but pity the boy who has never fired a gun; he is no more humane, while his education has been sadly neglected . . . Such is of-tenest the young man's introduction to the forest, and the most original part of himself. He goes thither at first as a hunter and fisher, until at last, if he has the seeds of a better life in him, he distinguishes his proper objects, as a poet or naturalist it may be, and leaves the gun and fish-pole behind" (212–13). At first I had the last line read "coming out a poet," but Thoreau doesn't really have the young man coming out of the forest as a poet; instead, he is going in again as a poet in later life. I'm not sure the last line in the revised version quite gets across the change in spirit, but it does rely more on image than statement.

fishing / sediment / sinking to the bottom "I have been surprised to consider that the only obvious employment, except wood-chopping, ice-cutting, or the like business, which ever to my knowledge detained at Walden Pond for a whole half day any of my fellow-citizens, whether fathers or children of the town, with just one exception, was fishing. Commonly they did not think that they were lucky, or well paid for their time, unless they got a long string of fish, though they had the opportunity of seeing the pond all the while. They might go there a thousand times before the sediment of fishing would sink to the bottom and leave their purpose pure; but no doubt such a clarifying process would be going on all the while" (213). The sediment sinking is obviously a natural image but also a suggestion of some sediment of mind that many bring to the pond. I love the summing up of fishing as a "clarifying process," which is only implied in the haiku version.

a hook of hooks / angling / for the pond itself Continuing from above: "The governor and his council faintly remember the pond, for they went a-fishing there when they were boys; but now they are too old and dignified to go a-fishing, and so they know it no more forever. Yet even they expect to go to heaven at last. If the legislature regards it, it is chiefly to regulate the number of hooks to be used there; but they know nothing about the hook of hooks with which to angle for the pond itself, impaling the legislature for a bait" (213). This is clearly metaphoric, but offers such an interesting rhetorical anomaly. What is this pond we go a-fishing for? I also like the implied pun and juxtaposition in *angle*, meaning "fishing" but also perhaps "straight lines meeting at a vertex," in contrast with the rounded circumference of a pond.

fishing less and less / a faint intimation / the first streaks of morning "I have found repeatedly, of late years, that I cannot fish without falling a little in self-respect. I have tried it again and again. I have skill at it, and, like many of my fellows, a certain instinct for it, which revives from time to time, but always when I have done I feel that it would have been better if I had not fished. I think that I do not mistake. It is a faint intimation, yet so are the first streaks of morning. There is unquestionably this instinct in me which belongs to the lower orders of creation; yet with every year I am less a fisherman, though without more humanity or even wisdom; at present I am no fisherman at all" (213–14). Thoreau goes on to explain his decision to give up eating meat. The abbreviated haiku version gives, of course, only the faintest intimation of the reason for giving up fishing. Again, the brevity of haiku highlights Thoreau's word choices and suggests further dimensions. The *faint streaks of morning* might echo the colors of a fish fresh from the pond. And that word *intimation*—meaning a "hint" or "suggestion" as he begins to see the light—perhaps echoes too the other *intimate*, to feel close to. And what is it that Thoreau intimates that he might feel intimate with? The morning, the light, the fish.

harvest of daily life / the tint of morning / a little star-dust caught "The true harvest of my daily life is somewhat as intangible and indescribable as the tints of morning or evening. It is a little star-dust caught, a segment of the rainbow which I have clutched" (216–17). *The tint of morning* perhaps harks back to *first streaks of morning* above. Try to catch that tint each day, instead of fish—it would be better for you. (Especially these days—there's no mercury in the sunrise.)

inspired through the palate / berries / eaten on a hillside "Who has not sometimes derived an inexpressible satisfaction from his food in which appetite had no share? I have been thrilled to think that I owed a mental perception to the commonly gross sense of taste, that I have been inspired through the palate, that some berries which I had eaten on a hill-side had fed my genius" (218). Maybe this is the secret of Thoreau's indefatigable and inspired journal-keeping: huckleberries! (What else might account for anyone managing to write that well every day?) Note again the possibility of wordplay. Thoreau is "inspired" in terms of artistic creation, but there is also the suggestion of intake, as in the process of respiration, where air is taken in. To Henry, the huckleberries too are one of the necessities of life.

jawbone of a hog / sound teeth and tusks / a creature that suc-ceeded "We are conscious of an animal in us, which awakens in pro-portion as our higher nature slumbers. It is reptile and sensual, and perhaps cannot wholly be expelled; like the worms which, even in life and health, occupy our bodies. Possibly we may withdraw from it, but never change its nature . . . The other day I picked up the lower jaw of a hog, with white and sound teeth and tusks, which suggested that there was an animal health and vigor distinct from the spiritual. This creature succeeded by other means than temperance and purity" (219). For all his praise of cleanliness and purity and morality in refraining from eating meat, Thoreau can still admire a carnivore that is often considered the epitome of slovenliness. This is nonjudgment and grate-ful acceptance.

a cool evening / the sound of a flute / stars over far fields "John Farmer sat at his door one September evening, after a hard day's work, his mind still running over his labor more or less. Having bathed he sat down to recreate his intellectual man. It was a rather cool evening, and some of his neighbors were apprehending a frost. He had not attended to the train of his thoughts long when he heard some one playing on a flute, and that sound harmonized with his mood. Still he thought of his work; but the burden of his thought was, that though this kept running in his head, and he found himself planning and contriving it against his will, yet it concerned him very little. It was no more than the scurf of his skin, which was constantly shuffled off. But the notes of the flute came home to his ears out of a different sphere from that he worked in, and suggested work for certain faculties which slumbered in him. They gently did away with the street, and the village, and the state in which he lived. A voice said to him, — Why do you stay here and live this mean moiling life, when a glorious existence is possible for you? Those same stars twinkle over other fields than these. — But how to come out of this condition and actually migrate thither?" (221–22). That's some flute playing. Interesting that the intellect as well as the spirit can be stirred by music rather than by rational discourse or argument. Haiku, ideally, has the same effect.

Brute Neighbors

keeping house / keeping bright / the devil's door-knobs "Why will men worry themselves so? He that does not eat need not work . . . And O, the housekeeping! to keep bright the devil's door-knobs, and scour his tubs this bright day! Better not keep a house" (223). This harks back to the lessons of "Economy" (make do with less) and *wabi* (cherish the value of material poverty). Note the pivot (*kake kotoba*) in line two. We initially read the first two lines as being parallel, so that *keeping house* is akin to *keeping bright,* which suggests that keeping house is a positive thing. But the final line requires us to reevaluate. *Keeping house* turns out to mean "keeping bright the devil's door-knobs." In other words, it is evil work. That shift is evident in Thoreau's original passage as well, but it is accentuated by the haiku format, where the space around line breaks adds both pauses and emphasis.

water from the spring / a loaf of brown bread / on the shelf "I have water from the spring, and a loaf of brown bread on the shelf" (223). Simplicity. Enough said.

those clouds / how they hang / nothing like it in paintings "Poet. See those clouds; how they hang! That's the greatest thing I have seen to-day. There's nothing like it in old paintings, nothing like it in for- eign lands, — unless when we were off the coast of Spain. That's a true Mediterranean sky" (223). Note that the "poet" (William Ellery Chan- ning), and not the "hermit" (Thoreau), makes the reference comparing nature to art. It would be in the spirit of haiku not to frame or perceive the natural world as a painting or other human construct. If anything, the haiku hermit would see even the human artifact as part of nature. But the idea that a view of clouds might be "the greatest thing I have seen today" — that is very much in the spirit of haiku. Perhaps that is the unspoken commentary on every haiku: "here's the greatest thing I have seen today."

meditation / shall I go to heaven / or a-fishing? "*Hermit alone*. Let me see; where was I? Methinks I was nearly in this frame of mind; the world lay about at this angle. Shall I go to heaven or a-fishing?"(224). Is that a pun on *angle*, a link to the idea of going fishing? I like how the haiku leaves ambiguous whether the choice is between meditation or fishing, or between two forms of meditation (going to heaven or going fishing). I am reminded of Jack Kerouac's haiku: "America: fishing licenses / the license / To meditate" (101).

whistle / for my thoughts / they have left no track Continuing from above: "If I should soon bring this meditation to an end, would another so sweet occasion be likely to offer? I was as near being resolved into the essence of things as ever I was in my life. I fear my thoughts will not come back to me. If it would do any good, I would whistle for them. When they make us an offer, is it wise to say, We will think of it? My thoughts have left no track, and I cannot find the path again" (224). Here is another nicely ambiguous phrasing: is Henry whistling for thoughts to call them back, or whistling because they are happily wayward thoughts? And isn't that the way of thoughts—to wander off without telling us where they're going or when they'll be back, if ever? There's your hound, bay horse, and turtle-dove.

red ants and black ants / their Battle of Concord / fighting for principle "One day when I went out to my wood-pile, or rather my pile of stumps, I observed two large ants, the one red, the other much larger, nearly half an inch long, and black, fiercely contending with one another. Having once got hold they never let go, but struggled and wrestled and rolled on the chips incessantly. Looking farther, I was surprised to find that the chips were covered with such combatants, that it was not a *duellum*, but a *bellum*, a war between two races of ants, the red always pitted against the black, and frequently two red ones to one black . . . It was the only battle-field I ever trod while the battle was raging; internecine war; the red republicans on the one hand, and the black imperialists on the other. On every side they were engaged in deadly combat, yet without any noise that I could hear, and human soldiers never fought so resolutely . . . I was myself excited somewhat even as if they had been men. The more you think of it, the less the difference. And certainly there is not the fight recorded in Concord history, at least, if in the history of America, that will bear a moment's comparison with this, whether for the numbers engaged in it, or for the patriotism and heroism displayed. For numbers and for carnage it was an Austerlitz or Dresden. Concord Fight! . . . I have no doubt that it was a principle they fought for, as much as our ancestors, and not to avoid a three-penny tax on their tea; and the results of this battle will be as important to those whom it concerns as those of the battle of Bunker Hill, at least" (228–30). Is this the broadest sort of anthropocentrism, and if so, is it deflating the human to ant level, or elevating ants to human level? Or is this some version of a principle of mutualism? We are like ants, and they are like us? Thoreau's interest in the activities of insects (family Formicidae) is reminiscent of Issa, though perhaps without Issa's compassion. Rather than interceding on behalf of any of the combatants, Thoreau remains the detached observer. Note the oxymoron in the idea of a "Concord Fight" or "Battle of Concord."

the woods ring / the hunter's wild discharge / the loon's wild laughter "In the fall the loon (*Colymbus glacialis*) came, as usual, to moult and bathe in the pond, making the woods ring with his wild laughter before I had risen. At rumor of his arrival all the Mill-dam sportsmen are on the alert, in gigs and on foot, two by two and three by three, with patient rifles and conical balls and spy-glasses. They come rustling through the woods like autumn leaves, at least ten men to one loon. Some station themselves on this side of the pond, some on that, for the poor bird cannot be omnipresent; if he dive here he must come up there. But now the kind October wind rises, rustling the leaves and rippling the surface of the water, so that no loon can be heard or seen, though his foes sweep the pond with spy-glasses, and make the woods resound with their discharges" (233–34). I took some liberty here by making the gunshots "*wild* discharges," mainly to find a quick way to suggest the errancy of their aim, but also to take advantage of the power of repetition in haiku, which becomes all the more effective in such a short space. But note the different connotations of *wild*—shooting wildly, meaning erratically, for the hunters, versus living or expressing oneself without bounds, in the case of the loon. In the passage Thoreau goes on to say that the hunters were not always so bumbling: "they were too often successful" in their loon hunting (234).

the surprise of fishes / a loon amid their schools / eighty feet deep "It is said that loons have been caught in the New York lakes eighty feet beneath the surface, with hooks set for trout,—though Walden is deeper than that. How surprised must the fishes be to see this ungainly visitor from another sphere speeding his way amid their schools!" (235). Thoreau too is loon-like in his ability to enter the world of the fishes here, to see things from their perspective. I toyed with making this one begin "visit from another sphere / a loon amid the fishes"—which adds a sci-fi touch and perhaps avoids the pathetic fallacy of attributing surprise to the fishes. But I like the image of fishes wide-eyed with apparent surprise, especially when the word *schools* leads us to imagine that these are young fishes as yet inexperienced in the ways of the world, underwater loons and all.

the loon looning / a long-drawn unearthly howl / the woods ring far and wide "His usual note was this demoniac laughter, yet somewhat like that of a water-fowl; but occasionally, when he had balked me most successfully and came up a long way off, he uttered a long-drawn unearthly howl, probably more like a wolf than any bird; as when a beast puts his muzzle to the ground and deliberately howls. This was his looning,—perhaps the wildest sound that is ever heard here, making the woods ring far and wide" (236). This is part of Thoreau's description of his game of hide-and-seek with the loon. A biologist friend tells me that the call described here is probably the loon's distress call. I wanted to use *this was his looning* as the first line, but the *his* lacked a referent.

Inserting *the loon* right before the verb *looning* clears up the reference problem, but it creates a repetition that is not in the original passage. It does, however, suggest something of the sound of the loon.

the stillness of the air / the smoothness of the water / the loon's long howl "Though the sky was by this time overcast, the pond was so smooth that I could see where he broke the surface when I did not hear him. His white breast, the stillness of the air, and the smoothness of the water were all against him. At length, having come up fifty rods off, he uttered one of those prolonged howls, as if calling on the god of loons to aid him" (236). Again, the sounds here are wonderful, echoing the subject and, I hope, highlighted by the haiku—the repeated rhythm of the first two lines, the *s*'s there, and the lengthy vowels and alliterated *l*'s in the third line.

House-Warming

a-graping / to the river meadows / beauty and fragrance and food
"In October I went a-graping to the river meadows, and loaded myself
with clusters more precious for their beauty and fragrance than for food"
(238). I have changed the sense of this, I suppose, by suggesting that the
"beauty and fragrance and food" are of equal value in Thoreau's assess-
ment of the grapes; the original creates a hierarchy of values with food
below beauty and fragrance. I love the verb *a-graping*. This is another
chapter-opening haiku moment, and again the passage opens with a
seasonal indicator.

*cranberries in meadow grass / plucked with an ugly rake /
jammed in Boston* Continuing from above: "There too I admired,
though I did not gather, the cranberries, small waxen gems, pendants
of the meadow grass, pearly and red, which the farmer plucks with an
ugly rake, leaving the smooth meadow in a snarl, heedlessly measuring
them by the bushel and the dollar only, and sells the spoils of the meads
to Boston and New York; destined to be *jammed,* to satisfy the tastes of
lovers of Nature there" (238). There may be too much judgment in this
one, but the shift in tone from line one to two is neatly reinforced by the
sounds (the "uck" and "ug" in the second line after the smooth flow of
the first). Notice the punning with *jammed*—overcrowded in the city,
jammed together, and, of course, made into jam.

the chestnut woods / sleeping their long sleep / under rails "When
chestnuts were ripe I laid up half a bushel for winter. It was very exciting
at that season to roam the then boundless chestnut woods of Lincoln,—
they now sleep their long sleep under the railroad,—with a bag on my
shoulder, and a stick to open burrs with in my hand" (238). This is all the
more poignant considering the loss of chestnuts in our forests because of
the chestnut blight, which arrived about fifty years after Thoreau wrote
this passage. Clearly the chestnut woods were already in decline from

overcutting in his day. Chestnut wood is very resistant to rot, which is why you can still find chestnut stumps in our woods today, and why it was chosen for such uses as fence posts and railroad ties.

scarlet maples / the character of each tree / reflected in the pond "Already, by the first of September, I had seen two or three small maples turned scarlet across the pond, beneath where the white stems of three aspens diverged, at the point of a promontory, next the water. Ah, many a tale their color told! And gradually from week to week the character of each tree came out, and it admired itself reflected in the smooth mirror of the lake" (239–40). Even without the calendar reference to "the first of September," the haiku makes clear the season. And the mirror metaphor is suggested and apparent even without spelling it out.

northeast shore in autumn / fireside of the pond / summer's last embers "Like the wasps, before I finally went into winter quarters in November, I used to resort to the north-east side of Walden, which the sun, reflected from the pitch-pine woods and the stony shore, made the fire-side of the pond; it is so much pleasanter and wholesomer to be warmed by the sun while you can be, than by an artificial fire. I thus warmed myself by the still glowing embers which the summer, like a departed hunter, had left" (240). This reminds me of Shakespeare's "That time of year thou mayst in me behold," with its comparison of a fire's embers and the arrival of fall—but without the third point of Shakespeare's metaphor, the comparison of both to the end season of a human life span. The haiku perhaps misleads by suggesting, with the image of embers in a fire, that the woods on the northeast shore are deciduous. I like the alliteration of the warm "m" sounds in *autumn, summer's,* and *embers.* Again, I find one of the benefits of finding haiku in *Walden* to be the highlighting of Thoreau's extensive use of sound devices.

studying masonry / to build my chimney / with second-hand bricks "When I came to build my chimney I studied masonry. My bricks being second-hand ones required to be cleaned with a trowel, so that I learned more than usual of the qualities of bricks and trowels" (240–41). I find this evocative in many ways—the conservationist ethic of "reduce, reuse, recycle" being put into practice, the value of reading (see chapter three), but also these existing in some sort of tension with the need to experience life freshly and at first hand.

mortaring the fireplace / our knives thrust into the earth / to scour them "I filled the spaces between the bricks about the fire-place with stones from the pond shore, and also made my mortar with the white sand from the same place. I lingered most about the fireplace, as the most vital part of the house. Indeed, I worked so deliberately, that though I commenced at the ground in the morning, a course of bricks raised a few inches above the floor served for my pillow at night; yet I did not get a stiff neck for it that I remember; my stiff neck is of an older date. I took a poet to board for a fortnight about those times, which caused me to be put to it for room. He brought his own knife, though I had two, and we used to scour them by thrusting them into the earth" (241). There is a neat pivot here, with the second line suggesting violence against the earth, which turns in the third line to reveal the earth as a cleansing force. And the materials for the fireplace come themselves from the earth.

the north wind / cooling the pond / a fire in the evening "The north wind had already begun to cool the pond, though it took many weeks of steady blowing to accomplish it, it is so deep. When I began to have a fire at evening, before I plastered my house, the chimney carried smoke particularly well, because of the numerous chinks between the boards" (242). Thoreau here pleasantly contrasts warm (retreating indoors to a cozy fire) and cold (the north wind, the pond in late autumn).

rafters with the bark on / where flickering shadows / may play at evening Continuing from above: "Yet I passed some cheerful evenings in that cool and airy apartment, surrounded by the rough brown boards full of knots, and rafters with the bark on high overhead. My house never pleased my eye so much after it was plastered, though I was obliged to confess that it was more comfortable. Should not every apartment in which man dwells be lofty enough to create some obscurity over-head, where flickering shadows may play at evening about the rafters? These forms are more agreeable to the fancy and imagination than fresco paintings" (242). The aesthetic of wabi is evident here. In an earlier version I had "flickering shadows / at play in the rafters / hermit's fresco," but rejected that on the grounds that the last line there is not fair either to Thoreau's meaning or to the spirit of haiku. It compares the shadows to an art form, but Thoreau specifies that the shadows are in fact different from—and superior to—a fresco. And in haiku, you try to see things for themselves rather than via comparison to a purely human frame of reference. Here is a case where I was tempted to introduce a metaphor where Thoreau in fact did not use one. Of course there's still an implicit metaphor in the idea of the shadows "playing" in the rafters. Though the fresco comparison is left out in the version I ended up with, I hope there is at least the implication of looking upward into the rafters by firelight and finding something beautiful and absorbing up there.

a house / which you have got into / when you have opened the door "My dwelling was small, and I could hardly entertain an echo in it; but it seemed larger for being a single apartment and remote from neighbors. All the attractions of a house were concentrated in one room; it was kitchen, chamber, parlor, and keeping-room; and whatever satisfaction parent or child, master or servant, derive from living in a house, I enjoyed it all . . . I sometimes dream of a larger and more populous house, standing in a golden age, of enduring materials, and without ginger-bread work, which shall still consist of only one room, a vast, rude, substantial, primitive hall, without ceiling or plastering, with bare rafters and purlins supporting a sort of lower heaven over one's head,—useful to keep off rain and snow; . . . a house which you have got into when you have opened the outside door, and the ceremony is over; where the weary traveller may wash, and eat, and converse, and sleep, without further journey; such a shelter as you would be glad to reach in a tempestuous night, containing all the essentials of a house, and nothing for house-keeping; where you can see all the treasures of the house at one view, and every thing hangs upon its peg that a man should use; at once kitchen, pantry, parlor, chamber, store-house, and garret" (242–44). The second sentence there, in its entirety, runs a full page, a sentence as commodious as the dwelling it describes. The haiku version is more on the scale of Thoreau's one-room cabin. Uncharacteristically for haiku, this one is not in the present tense but (what could be more fitting?) the present perfect.

sending home / each nail / a single blow "I did not plaster till it was freezing weather. I brought over some whiter and cleaner sand for this purpose from the opposite shore of the pond in a boat, a sort of convey-ance which would have tempted me to go much farther if necessary. My house had in the mean while been shingled down to the ground on every side. In lathing I was pleased to be able to send home each nail with a single blow of the hammer" (245). Such simple satisfaction in a job well done.

plastering done / the wind howls / given permission "At length the winter set in in good earnest, just as I had finished plastering, and the wind began to howl around the house as if it had not had permission to do so till then" (248). Note the sounds—the alliteration of the *p*'s in the first and last words of the haiku, the "un" sounds in the last words of lines one and three (*done, permission*), the assonance of the short *i* in *wind* and *given* and *permission* linking lines two and three—a sound structure withal. Again, notice that in the original passage, the seasonal reference is spelled out by way of introduction; in the haiku, the seasonal reference is sufficiently implied.

the wood-pile warming me twice / in the splitting / and on the fire "Every man looks at his wood-pile with a kind of affection. I loved to have mine before the window, and the more chips the better to remind me of my pleasing work. I had an old axe which nobody claimed, with which by spells in winter days, on the sunny side of the house, I played about the stumps which I had got out of my bean-field. As my driver prophesied when I was ploughing, they warmed me twice, once while I was splitting them, and again when they were on the fire, so that no fuel could give out more heat" (250). Here we see more of Thoreau's satisfaction in physical labor. Maybe he gets warm a third time, feeling a glow of satisfaction while admiring his wood-pile.

smoke from my chimney / gives notice to Walden vale / I am awake "But commonly I kindled my fire with the dry leaves of the forest, which I had stored up in my shed before the snow came. Green hickory finely split makes the woodchopper's kindlings, when he has a camp in the woods. Once in a while I got a little of this. When the villagers were lighting their fires beyond the horizon, I too gave notice to the various wild inhabitants of Walden vale, by a smoky streamer from my chimney, that I was awake" (252). Given the importance of waking throughout *Walden*, the claim of the last line of the haiku takes on added importance. In this case Thoreau makes his claim regarding his wakefulness to the wildlife with which he shares his place.

Fire and I / keeping house / moles nest in the cellar "My house was not empty though I was gone. It was as if I had left a cheerful housekeeper behind. It was I and Fire that lived there; and commonly my housekeeper proved trustworthy . . . The moles nested in my cellar, nibbling every third potato, and making a snug bed even there of some hair left after plastering and of brown paper; for even the wildest animals love comfort and warmth as well as man, and they survive the winter only because they are so careful to secure them" (253). Again, we see grateful acceptance on Thoreau's part, acceptance of the moles nesting in the cellar, taking advantage of the comforts provided by the human and the fire overhead.

a lamp / to lengthen out the day / a sharper blast from the north "The animal merely makes a bed, which he warms with his body in a sheltered place; but man, having discovered fire, boxes up some air in a spacious apartment, and warms that, instead of robbing himself, makes that his bed, in which he can move about divested of more cumbrous clothing, maintain a kind of summer in the midst of winter, and by means of windows even admit the light, and with a lamp lengthen out the day. Thus he goes a step or two beyond instinct, and saves a little time for the fine arts. Though, when I had been exposed to the rudest blasts a long time, my whole body began to grow torpid, when I reached the genial atmosphere of my house I soon recovered my faculties and prolonged my life. But the most luxuriously housed has little to boast of in this respect, nor need we trouble ourselves to speculate how the human race may be at last destroyed. It would be easy to cut their threads any time with a little sharper blast from the north. We go on dating from Cold Fridays and Great Snows; but a little colder Friday, or greater snow, would put a period to man's existence on the globe" (254). I was tempted to put the *sharper blast from the north* in line one, before the lamp lengthening the day, reversing the sequence so as to make the lamp-lit room seem a cozy retreat from the cold wind. But that rosy picture would not be quite true to the ominous note of Thoreau's passage, which emphasizes the power of the natural world to overcome our technology-based comforts. That ominous note seems all the more pertinent these days, what with recent human-induced alterations to our climate.

looking into it / at evening / always a face in the fire "It will soon be forgotten, in these days of stoves, that we used to roast potatoes in the ashes, after the Indian fashion. The stove not only took up room and scented the house, but it concealed the fire, and I felt as if I had lost a companion. You can always see a face in the fire. The laborer, looking into it at evening, purifies his thoughts of the dross and earthiness which they have accumulated during the day" (254). There's a twist on a familiar expression in the opening line: "I'll look into it," we say, intending to investigate a problem. But here the action in question is to stare at the fire that keeps us company.

Former Inhabitants; and Winter Visitors

evenings by my fireside / snow whirls wildly / without "I weathered some merry snow storms, and spent some cheerful winter evenings by my fire-side, while the snow whirled wildly without, and even the hooting of the owl was hushed" (256). Once again, a chapter opens with a strong image. The alliteration of the *w*'s suggests heavy wind.

my path through deep snow / oak leaves lodged in my tracks / melting them deeper "The elements, however, abetted me in making a path through the deepest snow in the woods, for when I had once gone through the wind blew the oak leaves into my tracks, where they lodged, and by absorbing the rays of the sun melted the snow, and so not only made a dry bed for my feet, but in the night their dark line was my guide" (256). Thoreau's keen observational skills are again evident here, along with his intense curiosity about how things work in the natural world—the things that most might not think twice about, like the effects of leaves gathering in footprints in snow. Rather than seeming a symbol of transience, the tracks in snow become deeper and more distinct.

a half-filled cellar hole / a fringe of pines / former inhabitants "For human society I was obliged to conjure up the former inhabitants of these woods . . . East of my bean-field, across the road, lived Cato Ingraham, slave of Duncan Ingraham, Esquire, gentleman of Concord village; who built his slave a house, and gave him permission to live in Walden Woods . . . There are a few who remember his little patch among the walnuts, which he let grow up till he should be old and need them; but a younger and whiter speculator got them at last. He too, however, occupies an equally narrow house at present. Cato's half-obliterated cellar hole still remains, though known to few, being concealed from the traveller by a fringe of pines. It is now filled with the smooth sumach

(*Rhus glabra*,) and one of the earliest species of golden-rod (*Solidago stricta*) grows there luxuriantly" (256–57). The tension here is built on the sadness and loss implied by lines one and three, on the one hand, and the hopefulness in that image of the fringe of pines, the forest renewing itself, on the other. In the prose passage, there is some humor in the white land speculator occupying "an equally narrow house"—a casket—as that of the dispossessed former slave. And there is humor too in Thoreau's ecocentric concern with naming the current botanical residents as well as the former human inhabitant.

apple trees / planted and tended by slaves / their fruit wild and ciderish "Down the road, on the right hand, on Brister's Hill, lived Brister Freeman, 'a handy Negro,' slave of Squire Cummings once,—there where grow still the apple-trees which Brister planted and tended; large old trees now, but their fruit still wild and ciderish to my taste" (257–58). Ironic juxtaposition is apparent in the fruit growing wild on trees planted by a slave.

a slave's epitaph / the date he died / telling me he had lived Continuing from above: "Not long since I read his epitaph in the old Lincoln burying-ground, a little on one side, near the unmarked graves of some British grenadiers who fell in the retreat from Concord,—where he is styled 'Sippio Brister . . . a man of color,' as if he were discolored. It also told me, with staring emphasis, when he died; which was but an indirect way of informing me that he ever lived" (258). This is a poignant—and pointed—indictment of slavery and racism. The uncharacteristic (for haiku) use of the past and past perfect tenses adds to the point about a life lost—lost even before Brister had died, perchance.

leaping the brook / in hot haste / to get to a fire "Breed's hut was standing only a dozen years ago, though it had long been unoccupied. It was about the size of mine. It was set on fire by mischievous boys, one Election night, if I do not mistake . . . I had just sunk my head [over a collection of English poetry] when the bells rung fire, and in hot haste the engines rolled that way, led by a straggling troop of men and boys, and I among the foremost, for I had leaped the brook" (259). The contrast, of course, is between the cool brook and the fire, and there is another pun in Henry's "hot haste" to get to the fire.

the nearness of the fire / our ardor cooled / no frog-pond to throw on it "The very nearness of the fire but cooled our ardor. At first we thought to throw a frog-pond on to it; but concluded to let it burn, it was so far gone and so worthless" (260). Thoreau offers here more contrasts of heat and coolness. The reference to the possibility of a fire-extinguishing frog-pond makes me want to ask "Where's Bashō when you need him?" I'm referring, of course, to Bashō's famous haiku about the old pond, the frog jumping, and the sound of water. I guess art can't always be relied upon to save us in times of crisis. But it also makes me wonder how firefighters in Thoreau's day would have gone about throwing a frog-pond onto a burning house. Bucket by bucket, I suppose.

former inhabitants / a dent in the earth / where hazel and sumacs grow "Now only a dent in the earth marks the site of these dwellings, with buried cellar stones, and strawberries, raspberries, thimble-berries, hazel-bushes, and sumachs growing in the sunny sward there" (263). All of our lives amount to little more than making a dent in the earth—a sense of fragility and the ephemeral is evident here. But raspberries, witch hazel, and sumacs are eternal—or at least perennial. Permanence and change—this is Bashō's aesthetic of *fueki ryūko*.

pitch pine where the chimney stood / sweet-scented black-birch / where the door-stone was Continuing from above: "Some pitch-pine or gnarled oak occupies what was the chimney nook, and a sweet-scented black-birch, perhaps, waves where the door-stone was" (263). The fact that it is *black* birch and *pitch* pine, with their suggestions of fire, adds to the sense of desolation—as in the opening few stanzas of Frost's "The Need of Being Versed in Country Things." Note the repetition of sounds (*p*'s, *b*'s, *w*'s, and *s-t*'s) and the nicely balanced rhythm here ("pitch pine where the chimney stood . . . black-birch / where the door-stone was").

still grows the lilac / door and lintel and sill / a generation gone
"Still grows the vivacious lilac a generation after the door and lintel and the sill are gone, unfolding its sweet-scented flowers each spring, to be plucked by the musing traveller; planted and tended once by children's hands, in front-yard plots,—now standing by wall-sides in retired pastures, and giving place to new-rising forests,—the last of that stirp, sole survivor of that family" (263). Here is the human artifact in decay (door, lintel, sill), while the lilac planted outside survives, reminiscent of Whitman's "When Lilacs Last in the Dooryard Bloom'd." Note the possible pun in *still grows*, which could mean that it continues to grow or that it becomes still and placid, a perception that perhaps indicates the observer's respect for the former inhabitants.

a path in deep snow / a dotted line / the same steps coming and going "In the deepest snows, the path which I used from the highway to my house, about half a mile long, might have been represented by a meandering dotted line, with wide intervals between the dots. For a week of even weather I took exactly the same number of steps, and of the same length, coming and going" (265). Here the real world takes on the semblance of a map. Thoreau seems aware of the oddity of taking the exact same steps on the same path, like stepping in the same river twice. Perhaps this image ties in with his later assertion that others have fallen into his path. Even he, by the necessity of deep snow, fell into a rut in his daily routine.

stepping in my own / deep tracks in snow / filled with heaven's own blue Continuing from above: "Stepping deliberately and with the precision of a pair of dividers in my own deep tracks,—to such routine the winter reduces us,—yet often they were filled with heaven's own blue" (265). The image of his steps filled with "heaven's own blue" puts a positive spin on Thoreau's repeated steps. The implication, perhaps, is that he sees something saintly in the way he is living his life at Walden. Plus, he is pointing out the phenomenon of deep new snow taking on a bluish hue.

the limbs of pines / drooping with ice and snow / sharpening their tops Continuing from above: "But no weather interfered fatally with my walks, or rather my going abroad, for I frequently tramped eight or ten miles through the deepest snow to keep an appointment with a beech-tree, or a yellow-birch, or an old acquaintance among the pines; when the ice and snow causing their limbs to droop, and so sharpening their tops, had changed the pines into fir-trees" (265). The second line suggests the snow is a burden crushing the spirit of the pines (and other venturers in the snow), but the language of the last line signifies something more positive. Read symbolically, the burden of the snow confers some clarifying result in the higher echelons of the human spirit as well as upon the conifers. The pyramidal shape implied here reminds me of Maslow's hierarchy of needs, and Thoreau's eye inclines to the high zone of self-actualization. I also like the quick dendrology lesson in Thoreau's passage here, giving information to help us distinguish firs and pines.

barred owl / launched off the limb of a white pine / feeling his twilight way "One afternoon I amused myself by watching a barred owl (*Strix nebulosa*) sitting on one of the lower dead limbs of a white-pine, close to the trunk, in broad daylight, I standing within a rod of him . . . At length, on some louder noise or my nearer approach, he would grow uneasy and sluggishly turn about on his perch, as if impatient at having his dreams disturbed; and when he launched himself off and flapped through the pines, spreading his wings to unexpected breadth, I could not hear the slightest sound from them. Thus, guided amid the pine boughs rather by a delicate sense of their neighborhood than by sight, feeling his twilight way as it were with his sensitive pinions, he found a new perch, where he might in peace await the dawning of his day" (266). Thoreau again demonstrates his skills as a good observer, or a good listener: the owl's silent flight is due to the rounded edges of its wings, an obviously useful adaptation for a predator that hunts at night. The assonance and internal rhyme in *white pine* and *twilight* puts extra emphasis on those words and might suggest the transition from light to dark, day to night.

wind on my cheek / heathen as I am / I turn the other to it "As I walked over the long causeway made for the railroad through the meadows, I encountered many a blustering and nipping wind, for nowhere has it freer play; and when the frost had smitten me on one cheek, heathen as I was, I turned to it the other also" (266). This is funny—Thoreau emulates true "Christian" behavior in turning the other cheek, but he makes the metaphor literal, and there seems something heathenish about his simply being out in the cold of winter. It is almost as if he dares the pagan gods of the elements to chill him, and in this case Christian doctrine serves him well—and offers quite practical advice.

tracks leading from my door / whittlings on the hearth / the odor of a pipe "Sometimes, not withstanding the snow, when I returned from my walk at evening I crossed the deep tracks of a woodchopper leading from my door, and found his pile of whittlings on the hearth, and my house filled with the odor of his pipe" (267). Note the sabi here—there is some haunting loneliness in the missed human encounter, a meeting only with the remnant fragrance of a visitor and his tracks in the snow, but also something beautiful in the observed details of whittled shavings and pipe odor, the evidence of a connection being made between neighbors even in their absence from one another.

visit from a friend / we make amends to Walden / for the long silence "The one who came from farthest to my lodge, through deepest snows and most dismal tempests, was a poet . . . We made that small house ring with boisterous mirth and resound with the murmur of much sober talk, making amends then to Walden vale for the long silences" (268). Again, sound repetition is rife here (*friend, amends,* and, more subtly, *Walden* and *silence*). I like the suggestiveness of the middle line, simply implying the nature of the sounds that make amends for the long silence.

over a dish of gruel / a bran new / theory of life "At suitable intervals there were regular salutes of laughter, which might been referred indifferently to the last uttered or the forth-coming jest. We made many a 'bran new' theory of life over a thin dish of gruel, which combined the advantages of conviviality with the clear-headedness which philosophy requires" (268). OK, admittedly the pun is terrible—let us all groan together. But it is only the second-worst, or perhaps I should say the second-most, overly ingenious pun of the book. My nomination for the best and worst is from "Economy," during the discussion of bread making. Thoreau speaks of the first strain of American yeast being brought over on the Mayflower, "its influence . . . still rising, swelling spreading, in cerealian billows over the land" (62). Cerealian / Cerulean—get it? Yeast rising? No? Oh well. In haiku, if not in polite society, puns are admitted and sometimes admired.

we sit and whittle / trying our knives / admiring the grain of the pine "Having each some shingles of thought well dried, we sat and whittled them, trying our knives, and admiring the clear yellowish grain of the pumpkin pine" (269). This reminds me of Thoreau finding in "Economy" that cutting the pines, rather than being a destructive act that leads to dissociation from the natural world, is a means of becoming better acquainted with them. Note the detailed description of the "clear yellowish grain of the pine"—a detail based on close observation that is somewhat surprising when you consider that the whittled wood is metaphoric. These are, after all, "shingles of thought" being whittled. The level of detail in the vehicle of the metaphor, clearly based on actual experience whittling particular pieces of pine and not just on the idea or general concept of whittling pine, suggests an interesting dimension to Thoreau's use of metaphor. Rather than render the natural object into nothing more than a symbol of an idea, the particularity of the descriptions of natural objects makes both image and idea fully present—and the image seems an equal partner in the metaphor, rather than subordinate to the idea it represents. The image's function in a Thoreauvian metaphor is to be something more than a representation of an idea, and to be fully present as itself.

fishes in the stream / coming and going / clouds float through the western sky Continuing from above: "We waded so gently and reverently, or we pulled together so smoothly, that the fishes of thought were not scared from the stream, nor feared any angler on the bank, but came and went grandly, like the clouds which float through the western sky, and the mother-o'-pearl flocks which sometimes form and dissolve there" (269). Here is a common technique of haiku: to take what otherwise might be expressed as simile or metaphor (this is like that) and to express it in the form of two juxtaposed images (this and that). Rather than say these are "fishes of thought" that float like clouds, haiku just says they are fishes, and we are left to think of all the other things that come and go like fishes in a stream or clouds in the sky—our lives, our loves, our thoughts, our moments of joy and sadness. Really, just about everything we know in this world.

there too / expecting the Visitor / who never comes "There too, as every where, I sometimes expected the Visitor who never comes" (270). Who is this mysterious winter Visitor? Friend or lover? Godot? The cable guy? Whoever it is, the waiting speaks to our essential aloneness, and again we see the spirit of sabi.

Winter Animals

Walden frozen / overhung by pines / bristling with icicles "When the ponds were firmly frozen, they afforded not only new and shorter routes to many points, but new views from their surfaces of the familiar landscapes around them . . . Walden, being like the rest usually bare of snow, or with only shallow and interrupted drifts on it, was my yard, where I could walk freely when the snow was nearly two feet deep on a level elsewhere and the villagers were confined to their streets. There, far from the village street, and except at very long intervals, from the jingle of sleigh-bells, I slid and skated, as in a vast moose-yard well trodden, overhung by oak woods and solemn pines bent down with snow or bristling with icicles" (271). I regret not being able to work Thoreau's skating into the haiku somewhere, but the image of the pines stuck with me most in the description. The quick dactylic rhythm of the last line and the repeated "s" sounds do convey some of the motion and sound of skating, though. For more on Thoreau's comments on skating, see my article "Winter Tracings and Transcendental Leaps: Henry Thoreau's Skating."

a hoot owl / the frozen earth / struck with a suitable plectrum "For sounds in winter nights, and often in winter days, I heard the forlorn but melodious note of a hooting owl indefinitely far; such a sound as the frozen earth would yield if struck with a suitable plectrum, the very *lingua vernacula* of Walden Wood, and quite familiar to me at last, though I never saw the bird while it was making it" (271–72). The word *suitable* makes the last line a bit long, but it seems an essential word. And of course this is highly metaphoric, comparing the earth to some sort of lute or acoustic guitar and the owl's hoot to a pick, but the image is provocative in its strangeness. A hoot owl seems at first more like a wind instrument than a stringed one, and the words *struck* and *plectrum* sound percussive, but somehow the odd descriptors fit with the fact that the call comes over the hard "frozen earth."

honking of a goose / the sound of wings / a tempest in the woods "One night in the beginning of winter, before the pond froze over, about nine o'clock, I was startled by the loud honking of a goose, and, stepping to the door, heard the sound of their wings like a tempest in the woods as they flew low over my house" (272). Auditory images prevail here. The reliance on nouns and prepositions seems typical of haiku. Each line follows the pattern of noun-preposition-noun, where the first noun is the subject and the second noun is the object of the preposition. Nouns are things, and prepositions show relationships between things (their position relative to one another). Things and things shown in relation to one another—that's not a bad summary of the content of haiku.

screech owl / responding to the goose / I too have lungs and a larynx "Suddenly an unmistakable cat-owl from very near me, with the most harsh and tremendous voice I ever heard from any inhabitant of the woods, responded at regular intervals to the goose, as if determined to expose and disgrace this intruder from Hudson's Bay by exhibiting a greater compass and volume of voice in a native, and *boo-hoo* him out of Concord horizon. What do you mean by alarming the citadel at this time of night consecrated to me? Do you think I am ever caught napping at such an hour, and that I have not got lungs and a larynx as well as yourself? *Boo-hoo, boo-hoo, boo-hoo!* It was one of the most thrilling discords I ever heard. And yet, if you had a discriminating ear, there were in it the elements of a concord such as these plains never saw nor heard" (272). Discordant elements unified in a harmonious whole—this the neoclassical writers termed *discordia concors*. (Or is it *concordia discors*?) Either way I detect another pun at work, since the clamor described by Thoreau as resolving into "concord" takes place on the outskirts of Concord, Mass. There is a universal here as well—many of us here on earth have in common lungs and a larynx, and we can all add to the chorus. I am assuming that what Thoreau calls the cat-owl is a screech owl, but it could be a barn owl, which also has a "harsh and tremendous" and somewhat catlike (if it was an angry cat) call. The barn owl's call is more of a shriek, actually, while the screech owl's call begins with a loon-like whinny. Being unsure, I went with *screech owl* in the haiku, since the name conveys the essence of the call Thoreau describes.

whooping of ice in the pond / restless in bed / and would fain turn over "I also heard the whooping of the ice in the pond, my great bed-fellow in that part of Concord, as if it were restless in its bed and would fain turn over, were troubled with flatulency and bad dreams" (272). In the passage it is clearly the pond that would (metaphorically) like to turn over in bed; the haiku leaves it ambiguous, so that we could read it as a human hearer who is kept awake by the sounds of the ice. But then the last line brings us back to thinking it may be the pond ice again that would fain turn over (since it would be odd to describe a person as ready and willing to turn over without his simply doing so). That pivoting effect is common in haiku.

squirrels on snow crust / in fits and starts / a leaf blown by the wind "All day long the red squirrels came and went, and afforded me much entertainment by their manoeuvres. One would approach at first warily through the shrub-oaks, running over the snow crust by fits and starts like a leaf blown by the wind, now a few paces this way, with wonderful speed and waste of energy" (273). Not only do the squirrels and leaves move in fits and starts, but we can also think of the snow, and by extension the seasons themselves, as entities that move in fits and starts.

squirrel in a pitch pine / chiding spectators / talking to the universe "For all the motions of a squirrel, even in the most solitary recesses of the forest, imply spectators as much as those of a dancing girl,—wasting more time in delay and circumspection than would have sufficed to walk the whole distance,—I never saw one walk,—and then suddenly, before you could say Jack Robinson, he would be in the top of a young pitch-pine, winding up his clock and chiding all imaginary spectators, soliloquizing and talking to all the universe at the same time, — for no reason that I could ever detect, or he himself was aware of, I suspect" (274). This is a syllable too long, another hyper-metrical haiku, but I couldn't bring myself to cut the word *pitch* in identifying the pine, because it puns on the pitch of the squirrel's chatter. Besides, the hyper-metricality seems apt given the squirrel's loquacity. Actually, a mammalogist friend tells me, the reason for the squirrel's behavior — the pause to look around, followed by the flurry of activity and chatter — is likely the presence of the human observer, a potential predator in the eyes of the squirrel. We've all seen this performance, of course, delightfully captured in Thoreau's brief description — and, I hope, in the abridged description of the haiku version as well.

squirrel on my wood-pile / thinking of corn / listening to the wind Continuing from above: "At length he would reach the corn, and selecting a suitable ear, frisk about in the same uncertain trigonometrical way to the top-most stick of my wood-pile, before my window, where he looked me in the face, and there sit for hours, supplying himself with a new ear from time to time, nibbling at first voraciously and throwing the half-naked cobs about; till at length he grew more dainty still and played with his food, tasting only the inside of the kernel, and the ear, which was held balanced over the stick by one paw, slipped from his careless grasp and fell to the ground, when he would look over at it with a ludicrous expression of uncertainty, as if suspecting that it had life, with a mind not made up whether to get it again, or a new one, or be off; now thinking of corn, then listening to hear what was in the wind" (274). Perhaps we all vacillate between a preoccupation with our various hungers and an interest in what news the wind might bring. But seeing the squirrel in a human frame of reference does not strike me as anthropomorphism; rather, Thoreau is describing behavior that we recognize as common to both squirrels and ourselves.

chickadees / faint flitting lisping notes / icicles in the grass "Meanwhile also came the chickadees in flocks, which picking up the crumbs the squirrels had dropped, flew to the nearest twig, and placing them under their claws, hammered away at them with their little bills, as if it were an insect in the bark, till they were sufficiently reduced for their slender throats. A little flock of these tit-mice came daily to pick a dinner out of my wood-pile, or the crumbs at my door, with faint flitting lisping notes, like the tinkling of icicles in the grass, or else with sprightly *day day day* or more rarely, in spring-like days, a wiry summery *phe-be* from the wood-side" (275). Lots of alliteration and assonance are at play here, in the *f*'s, *t*'s, *s*'s and the short *i*'s. Again, what Thoreau presents as simile (the chickadee calls "*like* the tinkling of icicles"), a haiku presents as a pair of juxtaposed images (the two images, chickadees calling and the "tinkling of icicles," set next to each other).

while I hoe / a sparrow alights / upon my shoulder Continuing from above: "They were so familiar that at length one alighted on an armful of wood which I was carrying in, and pecked at the sticks without fear. I once had a sparrow alight upon my shoulder for a moment while I was hoeing in a village garden, and I felt that I was more distinguished by that circumstance than I should have been by any epaulet I could have worn" (275–76). The hoeing that connects Thoreau to the earth has apparently repaired the separation of humans and humus, such that the sparrow sees no distinction between the human (this particular human, at least) and the natural. I pondered including the epaulet metaphor in this one in order to suggest Thoreau's pride at standing as a sparrow roost, and because the image of an epaulet might evoke the chevron shapes of a bird's wing and feathers. But I resisted, since the epaulet enters the sentence purely as metaphor, not as a directly perceived image.

in Walden woods a hunter / looking for a lost dog / finding a man "One day a man came to my hut from Lexington to inquire after his hound that made a large track, and had been hunting for a week by himself. But I fear that he was not the wiser for all I told him, for every time I attempted to answer his questions he interrupted me by asking, 'What do you do here?' He had lost a dog, but found a man" (277). Given the scarcity of men, as Thoreau might see it, capable of standing on their own two feet, we can understand the hunter's consternation at finding such a one as Thoreau. *Losing* and *finding* seem to be key terms in Walden—the hound, bay horse, and turtle-dove; the dog here; the thoughts he whistles for in "Brute Neighbors," those that have left no tracks; the self lost and then found in "The Village" ("Not till we have lost the world, do we begin to find ourselves" [171]). Perhaps the whole book is a description of what we have lost (among other things, our place in the natural world) and how we might go about finding all that again.

a roadside leaf / a hunter catching it / and playing a wild strain "The hunters were formerly a numerous and merry crew here. I remember well one gaunt Nimrod who would catch up a leaf by the road-side and play a strain on it wilder and more melodious, if my memory serves me, than any hunting horn" (279–80). The playfulness described here on the part of the hunter fits Thoreau as well—another one playing a wild strain in his life and in his writing. And haiku, of course, is full of play: with words, with images brought together in new and interesting ways, and with small things that are made to seem suddenly significant—things like making sounds by blowing edgewise on a leaf (a thick blade of grass works even better) held tautly in your thumbs.

a single mouse / a whole pine for dinner / its bark gnawed round "There were scores of pitch-pines around my house, from one to four inches in diameter, which had been gnawed by mice the previous winter,—a Norwegian winter for them, for the snow lay long and deep, and they were obliged to mix a large proportion of pine bark with their other diet. These trees were alive and apparently flourishing at mid-summer, and many of them had grown a foot, though completely girdled; but after another winter such were without exception dead. It is remarkable that a single mouse should thus be allowed a whole pine tree for its dinner, gnawing round instead of up and down it; but perhaps it is necessary in order to thin these trees, which are wont to grow up densely" (280). Here we see Thoreau, aided by his ability to take an ecosystemic perspective, arrive at a "grateful acceptance" of a natural fact that at first disturbs him. It initially seems such a waste that one rodent's repast should come at the expense of a whole tree, but then Thoreau sees that the apparent waste effectively thins the trees, allowing greater room and nutrients for those that remain and making for a healthier forest overall.

light-footed hare / *putting the forest* / *between us* "The hares (*Lepus Americanus*) were very familiar . . . One evening one sat by my door two paces from me, at first trembling with fear, yet unwilling to move; a poor wee thing, lean and bony, with ragged ears and sharp nose, scant tail and slender paws. It looked as if Nature no longer contained the breed of nobler bloods, but stood on her last toes. Its large eyes appeared young and unhealthy, almost dropsical. I took a step, and lo, away it scud with an elastic spring over the snow crust, straightening its body and its limbs into graceful length, and soon put the forest between me and itself,—the wild free venison, asserting its vigor and the dignity of Nature. Not without reason was its slenderness. Such then was its nature. (*Lepus, levipes*, light-foot, some think)" (280–81). I like the way the haiku calls attention to the phrase *putting the forest between us*, or, in the original passage, *between me and itself*. The familiar expression conveys the speed of the hare, but we are left wondering about nuances that underlie the expression's use here. Does the phrase suggest that the forest is itself a barrier of sorts between the human and the hare—such that even a Henry Thoreau can never really enter the woods where wild creatures live? Or are the woods shared ground, where he too has fled some potential threat?

a partridge bursting away / *as much expected* / *as rustling leaves* "What is a country without rabbits and partridges? They are among the most simple and indigenous animal products; ancient and venerable families known to antiquity as to modern times; of the very hue and substance of Nature, nearest allied to leaves and to the ground, — and to one another; it is either winged or it is legged. It is hardly as if you had seen a wild creature when a rabbit or a partridge bursts away, only a natural one, as much to be expected as rustling leaves" (281). And yet still, every time a grouse bursts from its ground cover, I am startled. This is the spirit of haiku: to take the "most simple" things that are "the very hue and substance of Nature"—those that are "allied to leaves and to the ground," things you may have seen many times before—and to find yourself startled by them once again. This is "beginner's mind."

The Pond in Winter

a still winter night / some question / has been put to me "After a still winter night I awoke with the impression that some question has been put to me, which I had been endeavoring in vain to answer in my sleep, as what—how—when—where?" (282). Again, Thoreau begins with a provocative chapter-opening line. The rhetorical anomaly here is in figuring out the equivalency of a still winter night and some ineffable question. Whatever the nature of that connection is, there is beauty in it. But the two parts of the haiku don't resolve—they simply continue to resonate. The haiku's open-endedness raises a question that the reader is left to figure out.

my morning work / I take an axe and pail / and go in search of water "Then to my morning work. First I take an axe and pail and go in search of water, if that be not a dream. After a cold and snowy night it needed a divining rod to find it" (282). This serves to illustrate the simplicity of wabi, evident in the action being referred to, the materials it is carried out with, and the language it is expressed by.

through a foot of snow / then a foot of ice / window at my feet "Standing on the snow-covered plain, as if in a pasture amid the hills, I cut my way first through a foot of snow, and then a foot of ice, and open a window under my feet" (282–83). The ice of Walden is not the easiest window to open, frozen shut as it is, but Thoreau offers no complaints.

kneeling to drink / I look into the parlor / of the fishes Continuing from above: "Kneeling to drink, I look down into the quiet parlor of the fishes, pervaded by a softened light as through a window of ground glass, with its bright sanded floor the same as in summer; there a perennial waveless serenity reigns as in the amber twilight sky, corresponding to the cool and even temperament of the inhabitants" (283). A confession—

after years of reading in "Sounds" that in Thoreau's day wood floors were polished with sand, I only now got the pun about the "sanded" floor in the "parlor of the fishes." I could not see a way to work that word-play into the haiku, though, without cutting the image of the speaker kneeling to drink and looking down. He seems almost godlike, looking down, but at the same time he is kneeling, like one who worships the pond.

heaven / under our feet / over our heads Continuing from above: "Heaven is under our feet as well as over our heads" (283). Taken literally, this means that the earth at our feet is as much a heaven as we can find in the sky above. But the contrasting *under* and *over* phrases are also familiar expressions. When we cannot find something we're looking for—in this case, heaven—we are told it's right under our own feet. But something that is "over our heads" means we are not capable of understanding it. The use of familiar phrases like this, brought back to their literal meaning while still reverberating with their metaphoric meaning, is one component of the lightness of language called karumi.

ah! the pickerel of Walden! / Walden all over / Walden all through "Ah, the pickerel of Walden! when I see them lying on the ice, or in the well which the fisherman cuts in the ice, making a little hole to admit the water, I am always surprised by their rare beauty, as if they were fabulous fishes . . . They possess a quite dazzling and transcendent beauty . . . They are not green like the pines, nor gray like the stones, nor blue like the sky, but they have, to my eyes, if possible, yet rarer colors, like flowers and precious stones, as if they were the pearls, the animalized *nuclei* or crystals of the Walden water. They, of course, are Walden all over and all through; are themselves small Waldens in the animal kingdom, Waldenses" (284). There is oneness here in the identification of the pickerel with their place, reinforced by the repetition, which becomes all the more powerful in the small space of a haiku.

with convulsive quirks / the pickerel give up / their watery ghosts
Continuing from above: "It is surprising that they are caught here,—that
in this deep and capacious spring, far beneath the rattling teams and
chaises and tinkling sleighs that travel the Walden road, this great gold
and emerald fish swims . . . Easily, with a few convulsive quirks, they give
up their watery ghosts, like a mortal translated before his time to the thin
air of heaven" (284–85). I love the *convulsive quirks* phrase, the sounds
of which nicely convey the feel of a sudden fish on the line. A quirk, my
dictionary tells me, is "an abrupt twist" as well as "an idiosyncrasy."

*stories told / of the pond's bottomlessness / they have no found-
ation* "There have been many stories told about the bottom, or rather no
bottom, of this pond, which certainly had no foundation for themselves"
(285). The pun is obvious—the stories have no foundation, because the
pond ultimately does. Notice the assonance: the long *o*'s in *stories, told,*
and *no,* the short *o*'s in *pond* and *bottomlessness.* There's also alliteration
in the *nd* of *pond* and *foundation.* In fact, the voiced and stopped "d"
sound, appearing in every line at about the same place (syllables three
or four), itself suggests a solid bottom. But note that lines two and three
end with a series of voiceless syllables, themselves a kind of bottomlessness, in not reaching a pronounced stop.

remarkable belief / the bottomlessness of the pond / unsounded
"It is remarkable how long men will believe in the bottomlessness of a
pond without taking the trouble to sound it" (285). Another pun—the
belief is as unsound as the pond is unsounded. Actually, the belief is
also unsounded as well as unsound—it has not been investigated very
deeply.

*the pond / deep and pure for a symbol / not an inch can be
spared* After Thoreau measures the pond's depth with a weighted line:
"The greatest was exactly one hundred and two feet; to which may be
added the five feet which it has risen since, making one hundred and

seven. This is a remarkable depth for so small an area; yet not an inch of it can be spared by the imagination. What if all ponds were shallow? Would it not react on the minds of men? I am thankful that this pond was made deep and pure for a symbol" (287). Every inch of the pond is as crucial as every word or morpheme in a haiku, which likewise seeks to achieve "remarkable depth for so small an area." Again, I am reminded of Bashō's old pond, its depths likewise unsounded, it too capable of reflecting the self or absorbing the self, it too unperturbed for all the attention paid to it and all the hot air that has passed over it, it too deep and pure and suggestive of so much else that is deep and pure, whether art, nature, or a life worth living.

one known fact / the bottom of the pond / the trend of its shores
"The regularity of the bottom and its conformity to the shores and the range of the neighboring hills were so perfect that a distant promontory betrayed itself in the soundings quite across the pond, and its direction could be determined by observing the opposite shore . . . Having noticed that the number indicating the greatest depth was apparently in the centre of the map, I laid a rule on the map lengthwise, and then breadthwise, and found, to my surprise, that the line of greatest length intersected the line of greatest breadth *exactly* at the point of greatest depth . . . If we knew all the laws of Nature, we should need only one fact, or the description of one actual phenomenon, to infer all the particular results at that one point . . . What I have observed of the pond is no less true in ethics. It is the law of average. Such a rule of the two diameters not only guides us toward the sun in the system and the heart in man, but draw lines through the length and breadth of the aggregate of a man's particular daily behaviors and waves of life into his coves and inlets, and where they intersect will be the height or depth of his character. Perhaps we need only to know how his shores trend and his adjacent country or circumstances, to infer his depth and concealed bottom" (289, 290–91). This rich idea, which Thoreau draws out over several pages, illustrates the transcendentalist claim that natural facts are symbols of spiritual facts. The scanty images of the haiku can do no

more than suggest the broadest outlines of Thoreau's argument—which, in essence, is what a map does, like the one of Walden that Thoreau includes amid this discussion.

wearing mittens / a prudent man cutting ice / to cool his summer drink "While yet it is cold January, and snow and ice are thick and solid, the prudent landlord comes from the village to get ice to cool his summer drink; impressively, even pathetically wise, to foresee the heat and thirst of July now in January,—wearing a thick coat and mittens! when so many things are not provided for. It may be that he lays up no treasures in this world which will cool his summer drink in the next" (293–94). We humans tend to devote so much of our lives to taking care of the future, and Thoreau is characteristically critical of that approach to life. The treasures we fail to stock up on may be those that can be captured only in the present (haiku) moment. But the image also contains some ambiguity—the "prudent landlord" is "impressively" as well as "pathetically" wise in planning for his cool summer drink. In the Japanese haiku tradition, coolness is often a supreme state of satisfaction.

ice-cutters / unroof the house of fishes / carting off their very air Continuing from above: "He cuts and saws the solid pond, unroofs the house of fishes, and carts off their very element and air, held fast by chains and stakes like corded wood, through the favoring winter air, to wintry cellars, to underlie the summer there. It looks like solidified azure, as, far off, it is drawn through the streets" (294). This is highly metaphoric (the "house of fishes"), but it features an intriguing shift in perspective by which we see the ice under our feet as the stuff from which fishes take their very breaths. I love the *solidified azure* phrase but, alas, could not find room for it in the haiku and decided that the idea embodied in that phrase is implied by the last line anyway.

taking off the only coat / the skin itself / of Walden Pond Regarding a massive ice-cutting operation one winter: "They said that a gentleman farmer, who was behind the scenes, wanted to double his money, which, as I understood, amounted to half a million already; but in order to cover each one of his dollars with another, he took off the only coat, ay, the skin itself, of Walden Pond in the midst of a hard winter" (294). This is shamelessly metaphoric, and judgmental too, and in those respects not typical of haiku; but it is also full of Thoreau's compassion for the pond. His anthropomorphism here can be seen as an attempt to grant the pond moral standing, in the same sense that Supreme Court Justice William O. Douglas once argued (in a dissenting opinion) that trees and mountains ought to enjoy legal standing.

the abode of winter / blocks of ice / packed in meadow hay "They stacked up the cakes thus in the open air in a pile thirty-five feet high on one side and six or seven rods square, putting hay between the outside layers to exclude the air; for when the wind, though never so cold, finds a passage through it will wear large cavities, leaving slight supports or studs only here and there, and finally topple it down. At first it looked like a vast blue fort or Valhalla; but when they began to tuck the coarse meadow hay into the crevices, and this became covered with rime and icicles, it looked like a venerable moss-grown and hoary ruin, built of azure-tinted marble, the abode of Winter, that old man we see in the almanac" (296). The interest here is in the conjunction of seasons—the ice of winter packed in bales of summer's meadow hay.

Walden water / reflecting clouds and trees / evaporating On watching the ice-cutters at work: "As often as I looked out I was reminded of the fable of the lark and the reapers, or the parable of the sower, and the like; and now they are all gone, and in thirty days more, probably, I shall look from the same window on the pure sea-green Walden water there, reflecting the clouds and the trees, and sending up its evaporations in solitude, and no traces will appear that a man has ever stood there" (297). Sabi and aware are evident here in the compassion expressed for our aloneness and for the ephemerality of all things. The works of humanity, the pond itself, they all evaporate, and our lives are as insubstantial as a reflection of clouds on the surface of a pond.

a solitary loon laughs / a fisherman's reflection / a floating leaf
Continuing from above: "Perhaps I shall hear a solitary loon laugh as he dives and plumes himself, or shall see a lonely fisher in his boat, like a floating leaf, beholding his form reflected in the waves, where lately a hundred men labored" (297). There is more sabi here in the images of insubstantiality, loss, and loneliness—note that all the images here are solitary. You could hear the loon's laugh as mocking; maybe he knows something we and the fisherman do not. But these images also convey quiet beauty. Even the loon's laugh might be seen as part of a pastoral pond scene.

the servant of Brahma / our buckets grate together / in the same well "Thus it appears that the sweltering inhabitants of Charleston and New Orleans, of Madras and Bombay and Calcutta, drink at my well. In the morning I bathe my intellect in the stupendous and cosmogonal philosophy of the Bhagvat Geeta, since whose composition years of the gods have elapsed, and in comparison with which our modern world and its literature seem puny and trivial . . . I lay down the book and go to my well for water, and lo! there I meet the servant of the Brahmin, priest of Brahma and Vishnu and Indra, who still sits in his temple on the Ganges reading the Vedas, or dwells at the root of a tree with his crust and water jug. I meet his servant come to draw water for his master, and our buckets as it were grate together in the same well. The pure Walden water is mingled with the sacred water of the Ganges" (298). Thoreau's grounding in both his home place and Eastern philosophy might account for the bent of his prose in *Walden* that makes it seem amenable to an approach via haiku aesthetics. The Buddha too sat by the Ganges. Whether or not haiku qualifies as a Zen art, it certainly is imbued with Asian philosophy and spirit—and, to some degree at least, so too is *Walden*.

Spring

after a cold night / my axe on the ice / resounding "One pleasant morning after a cold night, February 24th, 1850, having gone to Flint's Pond to spend the day, I noticed with surprise, that when I struck the ice with the head of the axe, it resounded like a gong for many rods around, or as if I had struck on a tight drum-head" (301). Isolating the word *resounding* in line three allows the word itself to resound — it evokes sound, and it suggests a small thing creating an unexpectedly large result, but it also perhaps takes on added significance in light of Thoreau's earlier "sounding" of the pond. Here is another way of measuring its depths.

the thundering of the pond / as surely as the buds / expand in spring "The fishermen say that the 'thundering of the pond' scares the fishes and prevents their biting. The pond does not thunder every evening, and I cannot tell surely when to expect its thundering; but though I may perceive no difference in the weather, it does. Who would have suspected so large and cold and thick-skinned a thing to be so sensitive? Yet it has its law to which it thunders obedience when it should as surely as the buds expand in spring" (301–2). What at first might seem a contrast between the pond's big booming and the buds' delicate expansion could also be taken as an echo of sorts, whereby the buds' expansion is as dramatic as the booming created by the ice's expansion, at least to a careful and dedicated observer.

bluebird, song sparrow, red-wing / the ice still / a foot thick "On the 13th of March, after I had heard the bluebird, song-sparrow, and red-wing, the ice was still nearly a foot thick" (302). Thoreau displays here his attentiveness to seasonal change — the kind of thing that in the last few years of his life led him to track in a daily calendar all the markers of seasonal change, from alterations in the ice to the reappearance of certain bird species and blossoms and fruits. The first line suggests the transition from the blues of winter to the warmer reds of summer.

the last of the ice / all gone off with the fog / spirited away Continuing from above, on the topic of ice: "As the weather grew warmer, it was not sensibly worn away by the water, nor broken up and floated off as in rivers, but, though it was completely melted for half a rod in width about the shore, the middle was merely honey-combed and saturated with water, so that you could put your foot through it when six inches thick; but by the next day evening, perhaps, after a warm rain followed by fog, it would have wholly disappeared, all gone off with the fog, spirited away" (302). We sense the spirit of sabi in the description of mysterious loss. As these last few chapters focus ever more intently on the physical world, here is a reminder of the mysteries of spirit. Where does the ice go? How does the fog effect its transference from one state to another?

a sullen roar the ice   drifting   to the shore On an old man duck hunting at Walden long ago: "He heard a low and seemingly very distant sound, but singularly grand and impressive, unlike any thing he had ever heard, gradually swelling and increasing as if it would have a universal and memorable ending, a sullen rush and roar, which seemed to him all at once like the sound of a vast body of fowl coming in to settle there, and, seizing his gun, he started up in haste and excited; but he found, to his surprise, that the whole body of the ice had started while he lay there, and drifted in to the shore, and the sound he had heard was made by its edge grating on the shore" (304). I've used the one-line form here. Japanese haiku, when printed in Japanese script, take the form of a vertical line; the breaks reflected in the three-line form we typically see in English translations are included in the vertical line. Many see a single horizontal line as a truer English adaptation of haiku form, and the horizontal line seemed a good fit for this description of ice drifting across the pond and arriving at the shore. The two images, the sound of the ice reaching shore and the visual image of it drifting, create a tension, the energy of a "roar" seemingly at odds with the placid movement of ice drifting. But the natural world does manage to incorporate both great energy and calm stability, discord and harmony, at every turn of the season. The rhyme is uncharacteristic of haiku, but does call attention to the sound at the heart of the haiku. The descriptor *sullen* at first struck me as too explanatory or figurative (projecting human emotion, it seems, to the reluctant ice); however, it raises an interesting rhetorical anomaly. Our eye, in fact, might tempt us to read it as a more customary "su*dden*" roar, and Thoreau may well be playing with, or against, our expectations regarding the word choice there. We are bound to wonder how a roar can be sullen, or why the speaker might perceive the ice in that way. Is it because the ice is seen as reluctant to touch the alien environment of land and to leave the liquid element from which it has arisen and to which it will return? The ice's solid state, we are reminded, is only temporary.

thawing sand / flowing down a bank / anticipating the leaf "Few phenomena gave me more delight than to observe the forms which thawing sand and clay assume in flowing down the sides of a deep cut on the railroad through which I passed on my way to the village . . . You find thus in the very sands an anticipation of the vegetable leaf" (304, 306). The thawing sand anticipates the leaf not only in form but also as seasonal marker.

the earth / expressing itself outwardly / in leaves Continued from above: "No wonder that the earth expresses itself outwardly in leaves, it so labors with the idea inwardly. The atoms have already learned this law, and are pregnant by it" (306). The earth expresses itself, but not in a form resembling human language. Rather than seeming anthropomorphic, then, the notion of an expressive earth suggests the possibility of our interacting with it—and the possibility of coming to understand what it has to say.

the feathers and wings of birds / the very globe / winged in its orbit "The feathers and wings of birds are still drier and thinner leaves. Thus, also, you pass from the lumpish grub in the earth to the airy and fluttering butterfly. The very globe continually transcends and translates itself, and becomes winged in its orbit" (306–7). The two juxtaposed images in a haiku usually echo each other in some way, suggesting an unexpected link. In this case, a bird and the globe are things not only capable of flight but also, as the reference to the feathers suggests, full of delicate textures.

the whole tree itself / but one leaf / and rivers vaster leaves Continuing from above: "Even ice begins with delicate crystal leaves, as if it had flowed into moulds which the fronds of water plants have impressed on the watery mirror. The whole tree is itself but one leaf, and rivers are still vaster leaves whose pulp is intervening earth, and towns and cities are the ova of insects in their axils" (307). The haiku doesn't explain the similarity of form in leaf, tree, and river, leaving it to the reader's participation to fill in the points of similarity and to perceive the unifying principle of vein, branch, tributary. Haiku is a poetry of suggestion.

thawing clay / the flow of fingers / the hand a spreading palm "What is man but a mass of thawing clay? The ball of the human finger is but a drop congealed. The fingers and toes flow to their extent from the thawing mass of the body. Who knows what the human body would expand and flow out to under a more genial heaven? Is not the hand a spreading *palm* leaf with its lobes and veins?" (307–8). The pun on *palm* (the tree, the palm of a hand) evokes the endless reiteration of the shape of veins and tributaries and appendages, the fractals of spring that add up to a universal form across a variety of scales of reference.

the Maker of this earth / but patented / a leaf "Thus it seemed that this one hillside illustrated the principle of all the operations of Nature. The Maker of this earth but patented a leaf" (308). This is both more metaphoric and more declaratory than haiku usually are. Indefensible, perhaps, as haiku—but I like it anyway. Even if the image is not particularly strong here, at least it leads you to think of images of leaves in trying to figure out what this statement is getting at. The quality of *yūgen*, then, is apparent.

this is the frost / coming out of the ground / this is Spring
Verbatim: "This is the frost coming out of the ground; this is Spring. It precedes the green and flowery spring, as mythology precedes regular poetry" (308). This is one of my favorites—so simple, bordering on wordiness with the (unnecessary?) repetition of *this is*, but still pointing to the ineffable, invisible essence that marks the change of seasons.

above the fossil earth / a living earth / the leaves of a tree "The earth is not a mere fragment of dead history, stratum upon stratum like the leaves of a book, to be studied by geologists and antiquaries chiefly, but living poetry like the leaves of a tree, which precede flowers and fruit,—not a fossil earth, but a living earth; compared with whose great central life all animal and vegetable life is merely parasitic" (309). The slight sound echo between *living* and *leaves* reinforces the image of the tree as emblem of the "living earth." The original passage, despite the disparaging comment on geologists, makes a case for the whole earth, geology included, as part of the living earth. Thoreau goes on to say, "You may melt your metals and cast them into the most beautiful moulds you can; they will never excite me like the forms which this molten earth flows out into." Those forms might mean whole landscapes as well as trees and leaves, all taking that same form of veins and tributaries.

frost out of its burrow / seeking the sea / migrating to clouds "Ere long, not only on these banks, but on every hill and plain and in every hollow, the frost comes out of the ground like a dormant quadruped from its burrow, and seeks the sea with music, or migrates to other climes in clouds" (309). This is quite metaphoric, but the idea of the moisture migrating to clouds and finding its way to the sea in spring—what a tidy summary of the hydrologic cycle. I use a haiku lesson in an interdisciplinary environmental studies class that I team-teach with a biologist, beginning the discussion with the idea that close observation of the physical world is a starting point of both haiku and the scientific method.

johnswort, hard-hack, meadow-sweet / the weeds Nature wears / through the winter "When the ground was partially bare of snow, and a few warm days had dried its surface somewhat, it was pleasant to compare the first tender signs of the infant year just peeping forth with the stately beauty of the withered vegetation which had withstood the winter,—life-everlasting, golden-rods, pinweeds, and graceful wild grasses, more obvious and interesting than in summer even, as if their beauty was not ripe till then; even cotton-grass, cat-tails, mulleins, johnswort, hard-hack, meadow-sweet, and other strong stemmed plants, those unexhausted granaries which entertain the earliest birds,—decent weeds, at least, which widowed Nature wears" (309). The pun, of course, is on *widow's weeds*, or mourning attire. A fair amount of alliteration is apparent here (*h*'s, *w*'s, *r*'s), and I like the falling rhythm of the first line—not as pretty in its sounds (which seems appropriate for weeds) but redeemed by the sweetness of the final species listed.

red squirrels under my house / deaf to the arguments / of boot heels "At the approach of spring the red-squirrels got under my house, two at a time, directly under my feet as I sat reading or writing, and kept up the queerest chuckling and chirruping and vocal pirouetting and gurgling sounds that ever were heard; and when I stamped they only chirruped the louder, as if past all fear and respect in their mad pranks, defying humanity to stop them. No you don't—chickaree—chickaree. They were wholly deaf to my arguments, or failed to perceive their force, and fell into a strain of invective that was irresistible" (310). Humor surfaces in the characterization of Thoreau's foot stamping as "arguments"—like James Thurber's classic line "Shut up, I explained."

Thoreau doesn't mention boot "heels," but I thought the monosyllabics of *boot heels* made a stronger statement than *stamping feet,* a sharper echo of the action being described.

the first sparrow! / faint silvery warblings / over bare fields "The first sparrow of spring! The year beginning with younger hope than ever! The faint silvery warblings heard over the partially bare and moist fields from the blue-bird, the song-sparrow, and the red-wing, as if the last flakes of winter tinkled as they fell!" (310). This is another one of my favorites, with beautiful sounds in *faint silvery warblings* and in the alliteration throughout (*f*'s, *s*'s, *b*'s). The images, both visual and aural, express the simple joy of seeing and hearing that first sparrow. The tone of the haiku reminds me of one of Issa's exultations: "Naked / on a naked horse / in pouring rain!"

marsh-hawk over the meadow / seeking the first slimy life / that awakes "The marsh-hawk sailing low over the meadow is already seeking the first slimy life that awakes" (310). I like the nonjudgmental attitude here—the hawk is as excited about spring as Henry is, and Thoreau seems to recognize their common bond in that regard. The fact that the hawk is out hunting is not held against it.

grass on the hillside / the rill out of the ground / spring fire "The grass flames up on the hillsides like a spring fire . . . as if the earth sent forth an inward heat to greet the returning sun; not yellow but green is the color of its flame;—the symbol of perpetual youth, the grass-blade, like a long green ribbon, streams from the sod into the summer, checked indeed by the frost, but anon pushing on again, lifting its spear of last year's hay with the fresh life below. It grows as steadily as the rill oozes out of the ground. It is almost identical with that, for in the growing days of June, when the rills are dry, the grass-blades are their channels, and from year to year the herds drink at this perennial green stream" (310–11). The fire image suggests both the warmth and swift spread of spring. The "rill out of the ground" at first seems unlike fire (cool vs. warm) until you think of it as moving like a flame. This description also makes me think of the "green fire" Aldo Leopold saw in his dying-wolf epiphany in the "thinking like a mountain" section of *A Sand County Almanac*.

a grass-blade / streams from the sod / into summer See above. This is another favorite of mine (among lots of favorites in these last two chapters). The grass grows so fast it resembles a stream, and as Thoreau describes more fully in the original passage, the grass-blade literally serves as a stream for thirsty cattle in the depths of midsummer, when the rills have dried up. The "s" sounds evoke both wind through grass and water in a stream. I love the idea of the grass streaming "into summer"—an unexpected twist there and an interesting rhetorical anomaly. How fast does that grass-blade grow? Right past spring and on into summer.

song-sparrow's chip-chip / from the bushes onshore / helping to crack the ice "Walden is melting apace . . . A great field of ice has cracked off from the main body. I hear a song-sparrow singing from the bushes on the shore,—*olit, olit, olit,*—*chip, chip, chip, che char,*—*che wiss, wiss, wiss.* He too is helping to crack it" (311). Did Thoreau intend the pun with the sparrow's chips, meaning its call but also "chipping" the ice away?

if I could ever find / the twig—*the twig*— */ the robin sits upon* "O the evening robin, at the end of a New England summer day! If I could ever find the twig he sits upon! I mean *he*; I mean *the twig*" (312). If I had to pick only one haiku from all of *Walden* to make the case that Thoreau had the soul of a haiku poet, this would be it. My absolute favorite. Like the best haiku, it defies explanation. But I'll try anyway. It says something, I think, about particularity, about noticing particulars, about wanting to see clearly and in detail, and it says something too about wanting words—like *twig* or *robin*—to be the things themselves and not representations of some other things.

the honking of geese / unrestrained complaint / mutual conso-lation "As it grew darker, I was startled by the *honking* of geese flying low over the woods, like weary travellers getting in late from southern lakes, and indulging at last in unrestrained complaint and mutual consolation" (312). This is perhaps a little too explanatory in interpreting the goose calls, but what a perfect explanation of the sound of geese. Perhaps *complaint* and *consolation* convey the purposes of most of our own language use as well. The mood of sabi and the repetition of sounds (the assonance of the long *a*'s in lines two and three, the alliteration of the *n*'s throughout) are wonderful.

geese spying my light / with hushed clamor wheel / and settle in the pond Continuing from above: "Standing at my door, I could hear the rush of their wings; when, driving toward my house, they suddenly spied my light, and with hushed clamor wheeled and settled in the pond" (312–13). The sounds in the middle line—long-drawn sounds, with stressed syllables close together slowing their progress—take a while to make it through the mouth. Then the final iambic line seems to settle into a more natural pace.

circling groping clangor / solitary goose / in the foggy mornings "For a week I heard the circling groping clangor of some solitary goose in the foggy mornings, seeking its companion, and still peopling the woods with the sound of a larger life than they could sustain" (313). Lots of "g" sounds here. What an unusual sequence of words in the first line, with its trochaic rhythm taken verbatim from the passage; the sounds themselves (*c*'s and *g*'s) seem to circle around.

plants spring and winds blow / to correct the oscillation / of the poles "In almost all climes the tortoise and the frog are among the precursors and heralds of this season, and birds fly with song and glancing plumage, and plants spring and bloom, and winds blow, to correct this slight oscillation of the poles and preserve the equilibrium of the season" (313). If I read this right, Thoreau is saying that the oscillation of the poles causes the change of seasons (that part is true), and nature's flurry of activity in spring serves to restore balance. This is fanciful science, perhaps, but the hyperbole makes for provocative poetry.

a single gentle rain / making the grass / many shades greener
"A single gentle rain makes the grass many shades greener. So our prospects brighten on the influx of better thoughts" (314). Thoreau's follow-up line spells out the moral dimension of the physical observation. Haiku leaves that to the reader.

the merlin's free / and beautiful fall / the earth lonely beneath it
"On the 29ᵗʰ of April . . . I observed a very slight and graceful hawk, like a night-hawk, alternately soaring like a ripple and tumbling a rod or two over and over, showing the underside of its wings, which gleamed like a satin ribbon in the sun, or like the pearly inside of a shell. This sight reminded me of falconry and what nobleness and poetry are associated with that sport. The Merlin it seemed to me it might be called: but I care not for its name. It was the most ethereal flight I had ever witnessed. It did not simply flutter like a butterfly, nor soar like the larger hawks, but it sported with proud reliance in the fields of air; mounting again and again with its strange chuckle, it repeated its free and beautiful fall, turning over and over like a kite, and then recovering from its lofty tumbling, as if it had never set its foot on *terra firma*. It appeared to have no companion in the universe,—sporting there alone,—and to need none but the morning and the ether with which it played. It was not lonely, but made all the earth lonely beneath it" (316–17). Beauty intermingled with loneliness—this is the spirit of sabi. The hawk's soaring and diving freedom is accompanied by separation from the earth. I have followed Thoreau's suggestion and called the hawk a merlin, or pigeon hawk, punning on the idea of a magician in the air. But its size and aerobatics indicate that it could also be a kestrel or a peregrine falcon.

tenant of the air / its nest in the angle / of a cloud "The tenant of the air, it seemed related to the earth but by an egg hatched some time in the crevice of a crag,—or was its native nest made in the angle of a cloud, woven of the rainbow's trimmings and the sunset sky, and lined with some soft midsummer haze caught up from earth? Its eyry now some cliffy cloud" (317). What a beautiful way of saying the hawk is at home in the air and seems a resident not of our common solid earth but of ethereal heaven. We do not usually think of clouds as sharp-angled or "cliffy," but it is true that they seem to take on landscape-like shapes.

wildness—where the bittern lurk / and the mink crawls / its belly close to the ground "We need the tonic of wildness,—to wade sometimes in marshes where the bittern and the meadow hen lurk, and hear the booming of the snipe, to smell the whispering sedge where only some wilder and more solitary fowl builds her nest, and the mink crawls with its belly close to the ground" (317). The sounds and images here are earthy, not lush or lovely. This, as opposed to the rainbowed terrain described in the previous haiku's source passage, is more commonly the territory of haiku. This justly famous passage—where Thoreau goes on to say, "We can never have enough of Nature . . . We must witness our own limits transgressed, and some life pasturing freely where we never wander" (318)—seems key to Thoreau's philosophy and worldview, and it very much allies him with the spirit of haiku. He does not try to prettify nature—he is cheered, for instance, by a vulture feeding on carrion or by the smell of a rotting horse—and he accepts it all (gratefully) for what it is, in all its rawness, in its wildness, a key word for Thoreau (see "Walking").

rambling into / higher and higher grass / on into summer "And so the seasons went rolling on into summer, as one rambles into higher and higher grass" (319). This image of the turning of the seasons as movement through space also appears in the earlier description of the grass-blade streaming into summer. Here the high grass reappears as an image of summer, with the movement of the seasons emblematized by the rambling human figure. Again we see the potential for effective repetition in haiku: in only nine words here, two are repeated (*into, higher*).

Conclusion

the wild goose / breakfast in Canada / lunch on the Ohio "The wild goose is more of a cosmopolite than we; he breaks his fast in Canada, takes a luncheon in the Ohio, and plumes himself for the night in a southern bayou" (320). Thoreau's strain of contrariety, his love of paradox, is evident here as he takes an emblem of the wild and heralds it as exemplar of the cosmopolitan, giving our human frame of reference a little shake-up.

bison keeping pace / with the seasons / going to greener grass Continuing from above: "Even the bison, to some extent, keeps pace with the seasons, cropping the pastures of the Colorado only till a greener and sweeter grass awaits him by the Yellowstone" (320). Thoreau's whole life at Walden might be encapsulated in the image of the bison here; he too is keeping "pace with the seasons" and finding "a greener and sweeter grass" at Walden's edge than that browsed by his contemporaries. This is reminiscent of Thoreau's admiration in "Walking" for those rare moments when domestic cattle give some evidence of their deep-down wild nature, "their native rights . . . their original wild habits and vigor"; he says that as they meander across a stream, they are "buffalo crossing the Mississippi," an "exploit which confers some dignity on the herd" (82).

stone walls around our farms / a universe wider / than our views of it Continuing from above: "Yet we think that if rail-fences are pulled down, and stone-walls piled up on our farms, bounds are henceforth set to our lives and our fates decided. If you are chosen town-clerk, forsooth, you cannot go to Tierra del Fuego this summer: but you may go to the land of infernal fire nevertheless. The universe is wider than our views of it" (320). Again we see that Thoreau likes to start chapters with a series of images; these first three are all from the first paragraph of the "Conclusion." Interesting that Thoreau is seen as the progenitor of nature writing's traditional emphasis on knowing your home place, but here he struggles against the implied constriction of boundaries. Something there is in Thoreau too that doesn't love a wall.

the West / our own interior / white on the chart "What does Africa,—what does the West stand for? Is not our own interior white on the chart? black though it may prove, like the coast, when discovered" (321). This haiku is heavy on metaphor, suggesting that the open and uncharted spaces of the West symbolize the soul. But it reminds me of the pun at the heart of Bashō's famous *Oku no Hosomichi*, or *The Narrow Road to the Deep North*. The place name *Oku*, often translated as "deep north," is sometimes translated as "the interior," meaning the wild backcountry (like the American West), but of course suggesting as well the human interior.

higher latitudes / empty cans piled sky-high / for a sign "Is it the source of the Nile, or the Niger, or the Mississippi, or a North-West Passage around this continent, that we would find? Are these the problems which most concern mankind? Is Franklin the only man who is lost, that his wife should be so earnest to find him? . . . Be rather the Mungo Park, the Lewis and Clarke and Frobisher, of your own streams and oceans; explore your own higher latitudes,—with shiploads of preserved meats to support you, if they be necessary, and pile the empty cans sky-high for a sign. Were preserved meats invented to preserve meat merely? Nay, be a Columbus to whole new continents and worlds within you, opening new channels, not of trade, but of thought" (321). The haiku extracted here remains mysterious about just what the cans might be a sign of. We were here, and this is our mark? The empty cans as the scat of a technological society? Help? Desperation? The higher latitudes, of course, refer literally to explorations in the Arctic and metaphorically to elevated pursuits of the mind and spirit. I think too of cairns on mountains above the tree line—marking the path, marking human presence—or of trash anywhere in wilderness. Actually, the original passage is pretty mysterious too. In the exploration-of-self metaphor, just what are the preserved meats and the empty cans? Are the preserved meats prepackaged spiritual sustenance available from one's culture, perhaps found in literature and history? Are the cans the attempts of desperate men before us who tried to leave a mark on the world?

a maggot / loving the soil / which makes our graves "Yet some can be patriotic who have no *self*-respect, and sacrifice the greater to the less. They love the soil which makes their graves, but have no sympathy with the spirit which may animate their clay. Patriotism is a maggot in their heads" (321). I thought about having the first line of this read "patriotism," using the sort of abstraction unusual (but not unheard of) in haiku, which would be truer to Thoreau's meaning here; he mocks love of country (or at least the idea of the country, if not the actual place) on the grounds that our country amounts to little more, in the long run, than a burial ground. Relying instead on the vehicle of the "patriotism is a maggot" metaphor makes a different poem, one more positively disposed to the maggot—and, for that matter, to the idea of our death as a natural process that is of benefit to the ecosystem.

an unexplored inlet / the Pacific Ocean / of one's being alone Continuing from above: "What was the meaning of that South-Sea Exploring Expedition, with all its parade and expense, but an indirect recognition of the fact that there are continents and seas in the moral world, to which every man is an isthmus or an inlet, yet unexplored by him, but that it is easier to sail many thousands through cold and storm and cannibals, in a government ship, with five hundred men and boys to assist one, than it is to explore the private sea, the Atlantic and Pacific Ocean of one's being alone" (321). Besides the ocean imaging loneliness, the *inlet* here puns on the idea of penetrating inward, soulward. Thoreau's cabin, by the way, stood near an inlet of Walden Pond.

a bark from the Gold Coast / out of sight / of land "It is not worth the while to go round the world to count the cats in Zanzibar. Yet do this even till you can do better, and you may perhaps find some 'Symmes'

Hole' by which to get at the inside at last. England and France, Spain and Portugal, Gold Coast and Slave Coast, all front on this private sea; but no bark from them has ventured out of sight of land, though it is without doubt the direct way to India" (322). Perhaps *Walden* is such a bark, showing us the route by which we can leave behind comforting shores and find our way to the unexplored "private sea." The selection of the Gold Coast as Thoreau's example of the safe place is particularly telling—and perhaps even more pertinent to the present day—since it serves too as an emblem of material wealth. Think of how thoroughly our culture assumes that economic prosperity is the highest ideal we, both as a society and as individuals, should strive for. Heaven forbid we protect any land or creatures if there is even the slightest economic cost involved.

day and night / sun down, moon down / and at last earth down too "Only the defeated and deserters go to the wars, cowards that run away and enlist. Start now on that farthest western way, which does not pause at the Mississippi or the Pacific, nor conduct toward a worn-out China or Japan, but leads on direct a tangent to this sphere, summer and winter, day and night, sun down, moon down, and at last earth down too" (322). Repetition, as in the repeated use of *down* here, takes on particular power in a haiku, which is of course short to begin with. Given so few words, to use the same word two or three times really calls attention to it. This passage provides an odd end to a paragraph devoted to the dictum "Explore thyself." Why all the downward emphasis? The point, perhaps, is that things still come to an end—they wind down—and discovering yourself will not change that. But to try to explore the self is a bold and worthwhile endeavor nonetheless, requiring courage (again, one of the characteristics Blyth stresses as key to haiku aesthetics) even, or especially, in the face of inevitable decline.

my path to the pond / the surface of the earth / soft and impressible "I left the woods for as good a reason as I went there. Perhaps it seemed to me that I had several more lives to live, and could not spare any more time for that one. It is remarkable how easily and insensibly we fall into a particular route, and make a beaten track for ourselves. I had not lived there a week before my feet wore a path from my door to the pond-side; and though it is five or six years since I trod it, it is still quite distinct. It is true, I fear that others may have fallen into it, and so helped to keep it open. The surface of the earth is soft and impressible by the feet of men; and so with the paths which the mind travels. How worn and dusty, then, must be the highways of the world, how deep the ruts of tradition and conformity!" (323). Another justly famous passage. The description of the earth as "soft" evokes comfort as well as environmental fragility. Note that Thoreau draws the moral lesson that the haiku leaves unspoken. But the mention of a path might well suggest further metaphoric dimensions even without his explanation, and the description of the earth as "impressible" might suggest that something more than a walkway is at stake here.

on the deck of the world / see the moonlight / amid the mountains
Continuing from above: "I did not wish to take a cabin passage, but rather to go before the mast and on the deck of the world, for there I could best see the moonlight amid the mountains. I do not wish to go below now" (323). Alliteration is featured here — *m*'s, mainly, but *t*'s and *d*'s as well. The last line in the prose version — "I do not wish to go below now" — suggests a metaphoric dimension: that he is not yet ready to leave this life and this beautiful world in order to "go below." Even without that interesting prose coda for the haiku, perhaps the sense of it is implied by the word *moonlight*; the moon appears at night, the end of things, but its light suggests the promise of things yet to come.

common sense / the sense of men asleep / expressed by snoring
"Why level downward to our dullest perception always, and praise that as common sense? The commonest sense is the sense of men asleep, which they express by snoring" (325). This passage contributes to Thoreau's guiding motif of sleep vs. wakefulness. Notice the pivot in the haiku version, which I think captures the humorous turn of the original

sentences: at first we perceive common sense as a positive thing, but that perception is undercut by the joke that the common sense we praise is nothing more profound or to the point than snoring. The alliterated s's echo the subject and sense of the passage.

the blue / of Walden ice / its obscurity "I do not suppose that I have attained to obscurity, but I should be proud if no more fatal fault were found with my pages on this score than was found with the Walden ice. Southern customers objected to its blue color, which is the evidence of its purity, as if it were muddy, and preferred the Cambridge ice, which is white, but tastes of weeds" (325). The metaphoric equation of the pages of *Walden* the book with Walden the pond anticipates the haiku by Ebba Story, quoted in the chapter on "Reading." I recall, too, Henrik Otterberg's recent book, *Hound, Bay Horse, and Turtle-dove: Obscurity & Authority in Walden*, which explores Thoreau's deliberate rhetorical use of the principle of obscurity. As Emerson says, all words, traced back far enough, have their origin in nature (he says that, of course, in his essay "Nature"). We think of *obscurity* as an abstraction, but Thoreau reminds us that it refers to a visual quality akin to opaqueness. Clearly many readers have charged *Walden* with obscurity. But in what way might that obscurity be considered "blue"? Those who consider *Walden* obscure also tend to see it as a downer, full of complaint and accusation. Others see it as a reflection of clear blue sky.

the mists / which envelop the earth / the azure beyond Continuing from above: "The purity men love is like the mists which envelop the earth, and not like the azure ether beyond" (325). This goes back to the whiteness of the Cambridge ice, mistaken for pure but really obscure in its cloudiness, versus the clarity of Walden's blue tinge. Note the implied dig at the received learning available at the center of higher education as opposed to the clear sight accessible to those who learn by experience. The haiku version does not necessarily invoke the discussion of ice, but the point still follows: most of us live in a cloud, but if we could get past it, we could reach the higher realm of the unclouded azure.

a man not keeping pace / the music he hears / far away "Why should we be in such desperate haste to succeed, and in such desperate enterprises? If a man does not keep pace with his companions, perhaps it is because he hears a different drummer. Let him step to the music which he hears, however measured or far away" (326). This famous passage works very much like a haiku in the lack of explanatory comment. The opening line perhaps suggests the context of someone choosing a road other than the one leading to Success by way of Enterprise. (Sounds like Amish country.) But from there the elaboration comes in the form of an image, with no follow-up comment or explanation. What follows is in fact another image—see below.

spring into summer / maturing as soon / as an apple-tree or oak "It is not important that he should mature as soon as an apple-tree or an oak. Shall he turn his spring into summer?" (326) In my previous readings of *Walden*, this was one of those lines I always glossed over after the quick thrill of recognition at the apothegm of the man marching to a different drummer. But now this follow-up image strikes me as very rich. I may have changed the meaning by shifting from the negative case—that is, that a man should *not* be in a rush to mature, or to leave spring so as to venture into summer—to the positive case, suggesting that maturation is as natural as the progress of the seasons or the growth of a tree, and that all these things happen in good time. Maturation, then, becomes a concept modeled by the turn of the seasons and the growth of a tree; it is the same action, modeled on different scales. But Thoreau clearly asserts a parallel between growth and maturation, on the one hand, and the progress of the seasons on the other. Further, the idea that we should not be in any rush to forsake spring for summer fits nicely with the pattern of the book, which begins in summer and moves around the cycle of the seasons to spring.

polishing a walking staff / Kalpa no longer / the pole star On the artist of Kouroo: "One day it came into his mind to make a staff. Having considered that in an imperfect work time is an ingredient, but into a perfect work time does not enter, he said to himself, it should be perfect in all respects, though I should do nothing else in my life . . . His singleness of purpose and resolution, and his elevated piety, endowed him, without his knowledge, with perennial youth. As he made no compromise with Time, Time kept out of his way, and only sighed at a distance because he could not overcome him. Before he had found a stock in all respects suitable the city of Kouroo was a hoary ruin, and he sat on one of its mounds to peel the stick . . . By the time he had smoothed and polished the staff Kalpa was no longer the pole star; and ere he had put on the ferrule and the head adorned with precious stones, Brahma had awoke and slumbered many times" (326–27). Just as the artist of Kouroo steps out of time by devoting himself to one project, so too does haiku aspire to timelessness. Partly haiku does that by capturing a single moment and holding it so that it does not dissolve into pastness. And partly haiku achieves timelessness by showing us the natural world and ourselves subject at the same time to both constancy and change, the immutable and the impermanent.

the artist of Kouroo / the heap of shavings still fresh / at his feet
"When the finishing stroke was put to his work, it suddenly expanded before the eyes of the astonished artist into the fairest of all the creations of Brahma. He had made a new system in making a staff, a world with full and fair proportions; in which, though the old cities and dynasties had passed away, fairer and more glorious ones had taken their places. And now he saw by the heap of shavings still fresh at his feet, that, for him and his work, the former lapse of time had been an illusion and that no more time had elapsed than is required for a single scintillation from the brain of Brahma to fall on and inflame the tinder of a mortal brain. The material was pure, and his art was pure; how could the result be other than wonderful?" (327). If one steps out of time while carving a walking staff or by becoming absorbed in the scent of a flower and the angle of the sun, what does it matter if one has stepped out of time for a moment or several millennia? Those are measurements in terms of that which has been transcended. The moonlight amid the mountains,

the azure beyond the clouds, the faraway music, the heap of shavings from the carving of a walking staff—all these are kept fresh and new in the magic box of a haiku. Or in a great book like *Walden*.

the setting sun / reflected brightly / from the windows of the alms-house "However mean your life is, meet it and live it; do not shun it and call it hard names. It is not so bad as you are. It looks poorest when you are richest. The fault-finder will find faults even in paradise. Love your life, poor as it is. You may perhaps have some pleasant, thrilling, glorious hours, even in a poor-house. The setting sun is reflected from the windows of the alms-house as brightly as from the rich man's abode; the snow melts before its door as early in the spring" (328). Here are the principles of nonjudgment and grateful acceptance. Nature, with all its beauties and satisfactions, is accessible to everyone, regardless of social or economic status. At the same time, note that it is a *setting* sun reflected so beautifully in the windows of the alms-house. That makes it all the more beautiful an image, but also adds the poignancy of sabi, for all our suns will set. That's what makes their beauty so poignant.

cultivating sage / sell your clothes / keep your thoughts "Cultivate poverty like a garden herb, like sage. Do not trouble yourself much to get new things, whether clothes or friends. Turn the old; return to them. Things do not change; we change. Sell your clothes and keep your thoughts" (328). The haiku highlights the pun on *sage*—worth cultivating as both an herb and wisdom.

a spider confined / to a corner of a garret / the world large "If I were confined to a corner of a garret all my days, like a spider, the world would be just as large to me while I had my thoughts about me" (328). The haiku leaves out Thoreau's qualifier that the world would be large as long as he had his thoughts. But the lack of that qualifier creates an interesting ambiguity in the haiku: is the spider a fool for being confined to a corner when the world about him is so large, or is even a corner of an attic world enough for any living thing?

a goose / a goose still / dress it as you will "I live in the angle of a leaden wall, into whose composition was poured a little alloy of bell metal. Often, in the repose of mid-day, there reaches my ears a confused *tintinnabulum* from without. It is the noise of my contemporaries. My neighbors tell me of their adventures with famous gentlemen and ladies, what notabilities they met at the dinner-table; but I am no more interested in such things than in the contents of the Daily Times. The interest and the conversation are all about costume and manners chiefly; but a goose is a goose still, dress it as you will" (329). The opening lines here suggest Thoreau's sympathy with the spider (above) confined to a corner of the garret. Is there a pun here on "dressing" the goose, as one would a turkey, with stuffing? The point clearly is that superficialities like "costume and manners" cannot cover up the essential reality of things. Note that the image of the goose encapsulates the essence of the discussion that precedes it—Thoreau's instinct to find a pithy image to sum up a concept is like that of a haiku poet or a writer of haibun.

a solid bottom everywhere / the horse sunk in a swamp / halfway there "There is a solid bottom every where. We read that the traveller asked the boy if the swamp before him had a hard bottom. The boy replied that it had. But presently the traveller's horse sank in up to the girths, and he observed to the boy, 'I thought you said that this bog had a hard bottom.' 'So it has,' answered the latter, 'but you have not got half-way to it yet.' So it is with the bogs and quicksands of society; but he is an old boy that knows it" (330). I created an end rhyme by changing *halfway to it* to *halfway there*, though rhyme is not typical of haiku—at least not since Harold Henderson's 1950s translations in *An Introduction to Haiku*. Henderson felt that rhyme might act as "a sort of frame to the picture" similar to the Japanese 5–7–5 *on* structure, which he considered "impossible" to duplicate in English (ix). In this case, my choice was dictated by my sense that *halfway there* had a familiar and colloquial ring to it that seemed to fit with the scene being described. And perhaps too the sound-echo suggests something of the idea of a solid bottom, with the horse in the middle line caught between the solid ground on the bog's shore and the solid ground below.

driving a nail home / a rivet in the machine / of the universe
"I would not be one of those who will foolishly drive a nail into mere lath and plastering; such a deed would keep me awake nights. Give me a hammer, and let me feel for the furring. Do not depend on the putty. Drive a nail home and clinch it so faithfully that you can wake up in the night and think of your work with satisfaction, — a work at which you would not be ashamed to invoke the muse. So will help you God, and so only. Every nail driven should be as another rivet in the machine of the universe, you carrying on the work" (330). Here Thoreau offers another paean to hard work, and of course the advice seems all the more credible coming from a man who built his own house, humble as it may have been. Add this to the list of Thoreauvian haiku that reverberate with the Zen-like suggestion that there is something spiritually satisfying about physical labor, whether it's waxing the car like the Karate Kid or fetching water like a holy man. The trick is to do well whatever you choose to do. I am also reminded of advice given by Thomas Foster in *How to Read Literature Like a Professor* (117). When you see a carpenter in literature, says Foster, think Christ figure, which makes all the more resonant the suggestion here that every smartly aimed swing of the hammer serves to build a better universe. Note how the prose passage first makes clear Thoreau's practical knowledge of carpentry, while the end suggests a wider and more spiritual dimension — the *yūgen*.

knowing a mere / pellicle of the globe / we delve six feet under
"We are acquainted with a mere pellicle of the globe on which we live. Most have not delved six feet beneath the surface, nor leaped as many above it. We know not where we are. Besides, we are sound asleep nearly half our time" (332). I'll save you the trip to the dictionary: a pellicle is the skin or rind of a fruit. I may have changed the sense of this in suggesting

that people *will* (or do) delve six feet down, whereas the original says they have not. But the six feet down brings to mind the grave, of course, and I cannot help but think that Thoreau chose that figure deliberately, planting the idea that though most have not yet delved that far down, their time to do so will come all too soon.

joy and sorrow / the burden of a psalm / sung with a nasal twang
"There is an incessant influx of novelty into the world, and yet we tolerate incredible dulness. I need only suggest what kind of sermons are still listened to in the most enlightened countries. There are such words as joy and sorrow, but they are only the burden of a psalm sung with a nasal twang, while we believe in the ordinary and the mean" (332). As a haiku, this at first suggests an un-haiku-like preoccupation with grand abstractions like joy and sorrow (that would be the *ga* section), but it is brought back to earth and the world of the familiar with the image of those big concepts sung in a "nasal twang." Though the prose passage ends with some scorn, the detail of the nasal twang seems to lend some compassion to the description.

water in the river / may flood the parched uplands / this may be the year "The life in us is like the water in the river. It may rise this year higher than man has ever known it, and flood the parched uplands; even this may be the eventful year, which will drown out all our muskrats. It was not always dry land where we dwell. I see far inland the banks which the stream anciently washed, before science began to record its freshets" (332–33). The haiku version leaves out the transcendentalist direction that we should think of the water as a metaphor for our lives. But notice how much Thoreau, for all the explanation of the spiritual dimension evoked by the natural fact, leaves open to suggestion. What are those muskrats that the rising water of our lives might drown out? Thoreau wants us to adopt a transcendentalist way of thought whereby all details of the natural world become meaningful, and he does not always point out just how each detail should be interpreted. Haiku, by virtue of its blank space, also encourages us to think of the implications, metaphoric and otherwise, of those closely observed details of the natural world.

an old kitchen table / of apple-tree wood / a bug gnaws its way out "Every one has heard the story which has gone the rounds of New England, of a strong and beautiful bug which came out of the dry leaf of an old table of apple-tree wood, which had stood in a farmer's kitchen for sixty years . . . —from an egg deposited in the living tree many years earlier still, as appeared by counting the annual layers beyond it; which was heard gnawing out for several weeks, hatched perchance by the heat of an urn. Who does not feel his faith in a resurrection and immortality strengthened by the hearing of this? Who knows what beautiful and winged life, whose egg has been buried for ages under many concentric layers of woodenness in the dead dry life of society, deposited first in the alburnum of the green and living tree, which has been gradually converted into the semblance of its well-seasoned tomb,—heard perchance gnawing out for years by the astonished family of man, as they sat round the festive board,—may unexpectedly come forth from amidst society's most trivial and handselled furniture, to enjoy its perfect summer life at last!" (333). Here Thoreau expounds upon the metaphor, preparing for the book's big rhetorical finish and hitting his keynote of waking and rebirth. Like a writer of haiku employing the aesthetic of wabi, he uses source images (the kitchen table, a hatching bug) that are humble and familiar.

more day to dawn / the sun / but a morning star "Only that day dawns to which we are awake. There is more day to dawn. The sun is but a morning star" (333). How poignant that the book ends with the start of day, reminding us to see the world with "beginner's mind," to see it freshly each moment, a new world before us each day. Ordinary things fraught with meaning—that's the spirit of *Walden*. That's the spirit of haiku.

Notes

1   In speaking of the tendencies of ecocriticism and nature writing, of course I generalize somewhat. In *Seeking Awareness in American Nature Writing*, Scott Slovic has suggested that nature writing does not in fact actually shift attention from the perceiver to the natural world. Rather, it reflects the *consciousness* of the perceiver, and what the writer seeks is not so much contact with the actual world as psychological awareness. And of course not all nature writing privileges solitude. For more on the social dimension of both nature writing and the haiku tradition, see my comments regarding "The Village."

2   The association of Zen with haiku is a contested idea these days. Blyth's assumption of the link has been long-lasting, though, as is evident by such works as Robert Aitken's *A Zen Wave: Bashō's Haiku and Zen* (1978) and Bruce Ross's collection *Haiku Moment: An Anthology of Contemporary North American Haiku* (1993). Ross's introduction stresses that "union with . . . nature" as "derived from Taoism, Buddhism, and Shintoism" is "at the heart of the haiku tradition" (xii). But recently the idea that haiku is inherently an expression of Zen principles has been challenged, perhaps most notably in George Swede's "Haiku in English in North America," Charles Trumbull's "The American Haiku Movement," and Haruo Shirane's *Traces of Dreams: Landscape, Cultural Memory, and the Poetry of Bashō* (1998). Swede and Trumbull point out that the American perception of a Zen dimension to haiku owes much to the influence of the Beats (foremost among them, as haiku practitioners at least, Jack Kerouac and Gary Snyder), who learned about the form primarily via Blyth's work. As is evident by my own commentary—and my references to Blyth—I'm in the camp that finds the perceived connection between Zen thought and haiku aesthetics fruitful and worth exploring further, though I would not insist on it as a necessary component of haiku practice. Lee Gurga, while noting that "the aesthetic ideals of haiku

are not uniquely associated with Zen" but are applicable to "any spiritual tradition," nonetheless notes that it is "useful and instructive to revisit Blyth's Zen-based aesthetic principles" (132, 128).

3   In a project that anticipates my tracing of haiku principles and language in the work of an American author, see Michael Dylan Welch's "The Haiku Sensibilities of E. E. Cummings." As I do with Thoreau, Welch, in addition to suggesting that haiku aesthetic ideas can be productively applied to an analysis of Cummings's poems, repackages some of Cummings's words in haiku form.

4   Earlier haiku texts in English referred to "onji" as the sound units of haiku, but *onji* is an archaic term no longer in use in Japan. For clarification on issues of "onji," "on," and morae, see Richard Gilbert's essay "Stalking the Wild Onji" in his study *Poems of Consciousness: Contemporary Japanese and English-Language Haiku in Cross-Cultural Perspective* (2008).

5   Though it's not directly relevant to my analysis of haiku as rheomode, perhaps an example of how Bohm works with verbs to develop his concept of the rheomode might be helpful. Thoreau's line "Let us not underrate the value of a fact; it will one day flower into a truth," originally from "A Natural History of Massachusetts" and quoted here in the "Conclusion," will serve as a useful demonstration. As it happens, the nouns *fact* and *truth* are two of the words Bohm chooses to analyze. His technique involves finding the essential action underlying an utterance and then working from there. The root of the word *fact*, he says, refers to "that which has been made (. . . as in manufacture)." So to "factate" is to make or do something, and to call attention to that making is to "refactate," and if it fits with the context it is "refactant." So essentially what we see as true is "something that 'works.'" But we always test what works, or what is deemed factual, and we of course are most interested in facts that seem constant. The word *constant* comes "from the Latin root 'constare' ('stare' meaning 'to stand' and 'con' meaning 'together')." So a fact remains constant if it is able "to 'stand up' to being put to the test." "Truth" comes from the Latin *verus* (as in "veracity"). To see truth is to "verrate"; to call

attention to what is true is to "reverrate"; and if it fits with what can be observed, it is "reverrant" (42–44). We might add that "value" is from the Old French *valoir*, or Latin *valere*, to be strong or to be of worth. Applying all this to Thoreau's quote suggests that he is interested in the strength or worth of facts not as fixed and static entities but as active agents that make or do something. If the reference is to natural facts, then his interest is in what nature makes or does. Facts that stand up to repeated observations may rise to the level of Truths, for which we may feel (and here's the transcendental pun) reverence. Or to keep it all in the realm of verbs: the strength and worth of nature are exhibited in what it makes or does, and when that making stands up to repeated observations, it is to be revered.

6   Spending just a few minutes with *Refuge*, I found these haiku as well, with page references for source passages:

>   whimbrels at the Refuge
>   a new thought
>   in familiar country (21)

>   Rain.
>   More rain.
>   The Great Basin is being filled. (29)

>   marriage maintenance
>   we drive to the edge of a lake
>   to watch birds (30)

>   hope—a roseate spoonbill
>   floating down from the sky
>   pink rose petals (90)

>   the wind rolls over me
>   sand skitters
>   across my face (109)

the wind picks up
   I hold my breath
      a raven lands (109)

a raven lands
   I exhale
      the raven flies (109)

a meteor flashes
   the waves hiss and retreat
      hiss and retreat (190)

Works Cited

Aitken, Robert. *A Zen Wave: Bashō's Haiku and Zen.* 1978. Washing-
    ton DC: Shoemaker & Hoard, 2003.

Barnhill, David Landis, trans. and intro. *Bashō's Haiku: Selected Po-
    ems of Matsuo Bashō.* Albany: State University of New York Press,
    2004.

Bishop, Elizabeth. *The Complete Poems, 1927–1979.* New York: Farrar,
    Strauss, Giroux, 1983.

Blyth, R. H. *Eastern Culture.* Vol. 1 of *Haiku.* Tokyo: Hokuseido,
    1949.

Bohm, David. *Wholeness and the Implicate Order.* London: Ark, 1983.

Buell, Lawrence. *The Environmental Imagination: Thoreau, Nature
    Writing, and the Formation of American Culture.* Cambridge, MA:
    Belknap Press of Harvard UP, 1995.

Cohen, Michael P. "Blues in the Green: Ecocriticism under Cri-
    tique." *Environmental History* 9.1 (2004): 9–36.

"Definitions." Haikupoet.com. 1 June 2006. http://www.haikupoet.com/.

Emerson, Ralph Waldo. "Experience." *Essays: Second Series.* Ed. Al-
    fred R. Ferguson and Jean Ferguson Carr, intro. and notes Joseph
    Slater. Cambridge, MA: Belknap Press of Harvard UP, 1983. Vol. 3
    of *The Collected Works of Ralph Waldo Emerson.* Gen. eds. Robert
    E. Spiller and Alfred R. Ferguson.

——. "Nature." *Nature, Addresses, and Lectures.* Vol. 1 of *The Col-
    lected Works of Ralph Waldo Emerson.* Ed. Alfred R. Ferguson.
    Cambridge, MA: Belknap Press of Harvard UP, 1971. 8–45.

——. "Thoreau." *The Norton Anthology of American Literature.* Vol.
    1. 2nd ed. Ed. Nina Baym et al. New York: Norton, 1985. 960–75.

Faulkner, William. "The Bear." *Big Woods: The Hunting Stories.* New
    York: Vintage, 1994. 9–97.

Foster, Thomas C. *How to Read Literature Like a Professor: A Lively
    and Entertaining Guide to Reading Between the Lines.* New York:
    Quill, 2003.

Gilbert, Richard. "Stalking the Wild Onji: The Search for Current Linguistic Terms Used in Japanese Poetry Circles." *Poems of Consciousness: Contemporary Japanese and English-Language Haiku in Cross-Cultural Perspective*. Winchester, VA: Red Moon, 2008.

Giroux, Joan. *The Haiku Form*. 1974. New York: Barnes & Noble, 1999.

Gurga, Lee. *Haiku: A Poet's Guide*. Lincoln, IL: Modern Haiku Press, 2003.

Hamill, Sam, ed. and trans. *The Narrow Road to the Interior and Other Writings: Matsuo Bashō*. Boston: Shambhala, 2000.

Hawthorne, Nathaniel. *Selected Letters of Nathaniel Hawthorne*. Ed. Joel Myerson. Columbus: Ohio State UP, 2002.

Henderson, Harold G. *An Introduction to Haiku: An Anthology of Poems and Poets from Bashō to Shiki*. Garden City, NY: Doubleday Anchor, 1958.

Johnson, Rochelle. *Passions for Nature: Nineteenth-Century America's Aesthetics of Alienation*. Athens: U of Georgia P, 2009.

Kawamoto, Koji. *The Poetics of Japanese Verse: Imagery, Structure, Meter*. Tokyo: U of Tokyo P, 2000.

Kennedy, X. J., and Dana Gioia. *An Introduction to Poetry*. 11th ed. New York: Pearson Longman, 2005.

Kerouac, Jack. *Book of Haikus*. Ed. and intro. Regina Weinreich. New York: Penguin, 2003.

Kullberg, Mary. *Morning Mist: Through the Seasons with Matsuo Basho and Henry David Thoreau*. New York: Weatherhill, 1993.

Lakoff, George, and Mark Johnson. *Metaphors We Live By*. 2nd ed. Chicago: U of Chicago P, 2003.

Leopold, Aldo. *A Sand County Almanac and Sketches Here and There*. 1949. New York: Oxford UP, 1987.

Lynch, Tom. "An Original Relation to the Universe: Haiku, Zen, and the American Literary Tradition." Diss. U of Oregon, 1989.

Marshall, Ian, and David Taylor. "A Catskills Dialogue: Looking for John Burroughs, from Wake Robin to Slabsides." *ISLE: Interdisciplinary Studies in Literature and Environment* 13.1 (Winter 2006): 167–81.

Marshall, Ian. "Winter Tracings and Transcendental Leaps: Henry Thoreau's Skating." *Papers on Language & Literature* 29.4 (Fall 1993): 459–74.

Otterberg, Henrik. *Hound, Bay Horse, and Turtle-dove: Obscurity & Authority in Thoreau's Walden*. Department of Literature Essay Series. No. 31. Gothenburg, Sweden: Gothenburg UP, 2005.

Phillips, Dana. *The Truth of Ecology: Nature, Culture, and Literature in America*. New York: Oxford UP, 2003.

Powell, Richard R. *Wabi Sabi for Writers: Find Inspiration. Respect Imperfection. Create Peerless Beauty*. Avon, MA: Adams, 2006.

Reichhold, Jane. "Haiku Techniques." *Frogpond* (Autumn 2000). Rpt. http://www.ahapoetry.com/haiartjr.htm. 5 January 2006.

Ross, Bruce, ed. *Haiku Moment: An Anthology of Contemporary North American Haiku*. Boston: Tuttle, 1993.

Shepard, Paul. *Coming Home to the Pleistocene*. Washington DC: Island, 1998.

Shirane, Haruo. *Traces of Dreams: Landscape, Cultural Memory, and the Poetry of Bashō*. Stanford, CA: Stanford UP, 1998.

Slovic, Scott. *Seeking Awareness in American Nature Writing*. Salt Lake City: U of Utah P, 1998.

Swede, George. "Haiku in English in North America." *Haiku Canada Newsletter* 10.2–3 (1997). Rpt. http://infinit.net/haiku/histnortham.htm

Taylor, David. "Giving Up on Language: Or Why I Quit Reading Thoreau." The Nature Writers of Texas. September 2003. http://texasnature.blogspot.com/2003/09/giving-up-on-nature-or-why-i-quit.html.

Thoreau, Henry. "Autumnal Tints." *Wild Apples and Other Natural History Essays*. Ed. William Rossi. Athens: U of Georgia P, 2002. 109–39.

——. *Journal. Volume 4: 1851–1852*. Ed. Leonard Neufeldt and Nancy Craig Simmons. Princeton, NJ: Princeton UP, 1992.

——. *Journal. Volume 8: 1854*. Ed. Sandra Harbert Petrulionis. Princeton, NJ: Princeton UP, 2002.

——. "Ktaadn." *The Maine Woods*. Ed. Joseph J. Moldenhauer. Princeton, NJ: Princeton UP, 1972. 3–83.

——. "Natural History of Massachusetts." *Wild Apples and Other Natural History Essays*. Ed. William Rossi. Athens: U of Georgia P, 2002. 1–24.

——. *Walden*. Ed. J. Lyndon Shanley. Intro. John Updike. Princeton, NJ: Princeton UP, 2004.

——. "Walking." *Wild Apples and Other Natural History Essays*. Ed. William Rossi. Athens: U of Georgia P, 2002. 59–92.

——. *A Week on the Concord and Merrimack Rivers*. Ed. Carl F. Hovde, William L. Howarth, and Elizabeth Hall Witherell. Princeton, NJ: Princeton UP, 1980.

Tripi, Vincent. *Haiku Pond*. San Francisco: Vide Press, 1987.

Trumbull, Charles. "The American Haiku Movement. Part 1: Haiku in English." *Modern Haiku* 36.3 (2005). Rpt. http://www.modernhaiku.org/essays/AmHaikuMovement1/html.

Updike, John. Introduction. Henry D. Thoreau. *Walden*. 150th Anniversary ed. Ed. J. Lyndon Shanley. Princeton, NJ: Princeton UP, 2004. ix-xxiv.

van den Heuvel, Cor, ed. *The Haiku Anthology: Haiku and Senryu in English*. 3rd ed. New York: Norton, 1999.

——. "Thoreau and the Haiku Spirit." *Frogpond* 27.2 (2004): 55–59.

Washington, Peter, ed. *Haiku*. New York: Everyman's Library, 2003.

Welch, Michael Dylan. "The Haiku Sensibilities of E. E. Cummings." *Spring* 4 (1995): 95–120.

"What Is Haiku?" *Logos & Haiku*. 1 June 2006. http://www. bekkoane.ne.jp/~ryosuzu/WHATHAIKU/html

Williams, Terry Tempest. *Refuge: An Unnatural History of Family and Place*. New York: Vintage, 1991.

Index

agricultural revolution, 138

aisatsu, 38

Aitken, Robert, 227n2

Allen, Woody, 138

alliteration, xxii, 60, 99, 119

"American Haiku Movement, The" (Trumbull), 227n2

animalizing, 128. *See also* personification

anthropocentrism, 102, 135, 140, 150, 169. *See also* ecocentrism

anthropomorphism, 190, 200, 204

Association for the Study of Literature and Environment (ASLE), xxiii

assonance, xxii, 60, 99

"Autumnal Tints" (Thoreau), xx

aware, xv, xxiv, 26, 69, 200

Barnhill, David, xvii, 38, 122

base section, 46, 50

Bashō, xiii–xiv, xix, xxiv, 14, 15; aesthetic principles of, 127, 181; as haikai poet, xxv–xxvi; definition of haiku by, 82; *Knapsack Notebook*, 100; *The Narrow Road to the Deep North*, xviii, 100, 133, 214; "old pond" haiku, xiii–xiv, 135, 153, 155, 181, 198; as writer of renga, 39

Bashō's Haiku (Barnhill), xvii

"Bear, The" (Faulkner), 93

beginner's mind, 11, 133, 194, 225

Bishop, Elizabeth, 93

"Blues in the Green" (Cohen), 94

Blyth, R. H., xxiv, 13, 15; attributes of haiku described by, xxiv; his assumption of haiku's Zen dimension, 13, 34, 103, 216, 227–28n2; his recommendation for haiku form in English, 141

—specific haiku attributes discussed: contradictoriness, 65; courage, 103, 216; freedom, 30; grateful acceptance, 56; materiality, 46, 56; non-intellectuality, 21, 34; non-morality, 53

Bohm, David, 91–92, 228n5

Buell, Lawrence, 75

Buson, xix, 15

"Catskills Dialogue, A" (Marshall and Taylor), 37

Channing, William Ellery, xx, 167

Cohen, Michael, 94

Coming Home to the Pleistocene (Shepard), 138

Concord, Mass., 120, 139, 169, 188

Confucius, 145

content links, 39–40

coolness, 199

Cummings, E. E., 228n3

dendrology, 183

Derrida, Jacques, 111

Dharma Bums, The (Kerouac), 94

discordia concors, 188

Douglas, William O., 200

ecocentrism, 75, 94, 137–38, 150, 180

ecocriticism, xxiii–xxv, xxviii, 94, 227n1

ecology, 40–41, 64

ecotone, 115

egolessness, xiv, 6, 143

Eliot, T. S., 121

Emerson, Ralph Waldo, 64, 76, 89; "Experience," xxi; "Nature," 47, 56, 120, 218

"Experience" (Emerson), xxi

Faulkner, William, 93
Fish, Stanley, xxix
"Fish, The" (Bishop), 93
Foster, Thomas, 223
found haiku, xxviii–xxix, 75, 95
Frogpond, xxvi
Frost, Robert, 181
fueki ryōko, 181

ga, 46–47, 224
Gandhi, Mahatma, 144
Gilbert, Richard, 228n4
"Giving Up on Language" (Taylor), 37
grateful acceptance, 56; of carnivores, 165; of the conditions of life, 106, 115; of disturbing natural facts, 193; of moles, 177; of the railroad, 119; of social status, 221; of whatever the earth gives, 135, 138; wherever you are, 159; of wildness, 212; of the world, 124. *See also* Blyth, R. H.
Gurga, Lee, xxi, 6–7, 50, 69, 227n2

Haeckel, Ernst, 41
haibun, xviii, 14, 94, 100, 148
haijin, xxvi
Haiku (Blyth), xxiv, 13
haiku aesthetics: applied to non-haiku poets, 228n3; coolness, 199; formal qualities of, 38; introduced, xvii; Kawamoto's discussion of, 46, 50; pertinence to ecocriticism and nature writing, xxiii–xxvii, 94; pertinence to Thoreau and *Walden*, xvi–xviii, xxiii–xxvii, 10–11, 14–15, 99–101, 201; as poetics of the ordinary, 105; and Zen thought 227–28n2. *See also* Blyth, R. H.; Japanese literary aesthetics, conventions of; Japanese literary devices; Kawamoto; language registers; *waka*

—concepts of: beginner's mind (ability to see things innocently and directly, simplification), 11, 133, 194, 225; egolessness, xiv, 6, 143; *yōgen* (depth of meaning and resonance in a haiku), xx, 47, 69, 73, 89, 95; *yōgen* in particular haiku, 149, 206, 223
haiku index, 94
"Haiku in English in North America" (Swede), 227n2
Haiku Moment (Ross), 227n2
Haiku Pond (Tripi), 16
"Haiku Sensibilities of E. E. Cummings, The" (Welch), 228n3
Hamill, Sam, 26
Hawthorne, Nathaniel, 64
Henderson, Harold, 222
hierarchy of needs (Maslow), 132, 183
History of Haiku (Blyth), xxiv
hokku, xxv, 38
honkadori, 16
hosomi, xxiv, 5–7, 89, 109
Hound, Bay Horse, and Turtle-dove (Otterberg), 104, 218
How to Read Literature Like a Professor (Foster), 223
hydrologic cycle, 148, 207
hyperbole, 50, 130, 211
hyper-metricality, 141, 190

intentional fallacy, xxvii
Introduction to Haiku, An (Henderson), 222
Issa, xix, 15, 208; insects as his subject, 109, 134, 169; *The Spring of My Life*, 100

Japanese literary aesthetics, conventions of, xxiv; *aware*, xv, xxiv, 26, 69, 200; *hosomi*, xxiv, 5–7, 89, 109; *karumi*, xv, xxiv, 35, 68–69, 89, 99, 109, 127, 196; *sabi* (defined), xvii, xxiv, 26, 127, 211; *sabi* in particular haiku, 69, 121, 123, 186, 200, 201, 203; *shibumi*, xxiv, 7, 89, 99; *wabi*, xv, xxiv, 95, 109, 130–31, 167, 175, 195, 225; *wabi* and Thoreau, 10–11, 89, 99, 102, 106. *See also* haiku aesthetics

Japanese literary devices: *honkadori*, 16; hyperbole, 50, 130, 211; *kake kotoba*, 167; pivot words, 151, 167, 174, 189, 217; puns as pivot words, 34, 159. *See also* Japanese literary aesthetics, conventions of

ji-amari, 141

Johnson, Mark, 73

Johnson, Rochelle, 74–75

Journal (Thoreau), xiv, xv, xix

kake kotoba, 167. *See also* pivot words

Kalendar project (Thoreau), 74, 90, 202

karumi, xv, xxiv, 35, 68–69, 89, 99; in particular haiku, 109, 127, 196

Katahdin, Mt., 7

Kawamoto, Koji, 38, 46, 50, 141

Kerouac, Jack, 94, 168, 227n2

kigo, 46

King, Martin Luther, Jr., 144

Knapsack Notebook (Bashō), 100

koan, 75, 102

"Ktaadn" (Thoreau), 7, 89

Kullberg, Mary, 14

Lakoff, George, 73

language registers (in haiku): *ga*, 46–47, 224; *kigo*, 46; *renga*, xxv, 38–41; *zoku*, 46–47

Leopold, Aldo, 93, 209

lexical links, 39–40

Lynch, Tom, 15

Marshall, Ian, 37, 187

Maslow, Abraham, 132, 183

materiality, 46, 56

metaphor, 47, 75, 199, 200, 206, 215; associated with transcendentalism, xv, 47, 73, 89–90; defended, 152, 153; implied by a haiku, 173, 175, 217; juxtaposition and, 156, 186; meaning spelled out, 225; omitted in the haiku, 104, 128, 130, 149–50, 191; rhetorical anomaly and, 163, 187; retention of, defended, 152, 153; in Thoreau's writing, xxiii, 73–75, 128, 149–50, 185–86; typically avoided in haiku, xv, xix, 73,110, 200, 206

Modern Haiku, xxvi, 13

morae, 38, 140, 228n4

Morning Mist (Kullberg), 14

Narrow Road to the Deep North, The (Bashō), xviii, 100, 133, 214

"Natural History of Massachusetts, A" (Thoreau), 89, 228n5

"Nature" (Emerson), 47, 56, 120, 218

nature writing, xiii, xiv, xxiii–xxvii, 93–95, 227n1; emphasis on home place, 214; social dimensions of, 37

"Need of Being Versed in Country Things, The" (Frost), 181

New Criticism, xxvii–xxviii

non-intellectuality, xv, 21, 34–35

nonjudgment, 117, 165, 208, 221

non-morality, 53

objective correlative, 121

on, 38, 140, 222, 228n4

"Original Relation to the Universe, An" (Lynch), 15

Otterberg, Henrik, 104, 218

oxymoron, 169

paradox: as element of haiku aesthetics, xv, 64–65; as element of Thoreau's style, xv, 64–65, 102, 106, 144, 213; as a form of rhetorical anomaly, 50, 100, 162

pathetic fallacy, 121
personification: omitted in the haiku, 150, 151; retained in the haiku, 47, 134; reverse personification, 128; as rhetorical anomaly, 135, 137; typically avoided in haiku, 47
Petrulionis, Sandy, xv
Phillips, Dana, 94
phonocentrism, 111
pivot words, 151, 167, 174, 189, 217; puns as, 34, 159
Poems of Consciousness (Gilbert), 228n4
Poetics of Japanese Verse, The (Kawamoto), 46
Powell, Richard, 10
present, 14, 82–83, 90, 111, 199
present tense, xvii, 92, 176
puns: the best/worst in *Walden*, 185; as element of haiku aesthetics, xvi, 34–35, 46, 110; as element of Thoreau's style, xxii–xxiii, 34–35; highlighted by the haiku, 221; highlighting key words, 119, 132, 137, 163, 188; omitted from the haiku, 118, 196; as pivot words, 159; possible, 103, 126, 165, 209, 222; as rhetorical anomaly, 50, 100

quantitative meter, 140

reader-response theory, xxix
"Red Wheelbarrow, The" (W. C. Williams), 123
Refuge (T. T. Williams), 94, 229–30n6
Reichhold, Jane, 26
renga, xxv, 38–41
"Resistance to Civil Government" (Thoreau), 144
rheomode, 91–92, 228n5
rhetorical anomaly, 99, 195, 209; defined, 50; disrupted syntax as, 103; forms of, 50; metaphor as, 163;

paradox as, 162; personification as, 135, 137, 204; sound devices as, 60; in Thoreau's prose, 50, 99–100. *See also* hyperbole; metaphor; paradox; personification; sound devices
rhyme, 60, 118–19, 222
Ross, Bruce, 16, 227n2

sabi, 186, 203; ambiguity of, 26; associated with compassion, 26, 200; defined, xvii, xxiv, 26–27; mingling beauty and loneliness, 201, 211; mood of, 123; paradoxical quality of, 127; poignancy of, 121; source of depth, 69; in Thoreau's prose, 26–27, 89
sampling, 101
Sand County Almanac, A (Leopold), 93, 209
Sanders, Scott Russell, 37
scent links, 39–40
seasonal awareness, xix, xxviii, 13–14, 93, 109, 200
seasonal change, 189, 212; central to haiku, 82, 93; as framework for *Walden*, 40, 82, 93, 122, 219; maturation compared to, 219; oscillation of the poles and, 210; Thoreau's attentiveness to, xiii, xxviii, 202
seasonal reference, 83, 123, 172, 204; holidays as, 109; implied, 173, 176; as "meaning-making hint," 46; in renga, 38. See also *kigo*
Seeking Awareness in American Nature Writing (Slovic), 227n1
senryō, 109
Shakespeare, William, 173
Shepard, Paul, 138
shibumi, xxiv, 7, 89, 99
Shiki, xxvi, 15
Shirane, Haruo, 227n2
Slovic, Scott, 82, 227n1
Snyder, Gary, 227n2

sound devices, xxi, xxii, 60, 99, 100, 173. *See also* alliteration; rhyme
"Speculations" (Spiess), 13
Spiess, Robert, 13–14
Spring of My Life, The (Issa), 100
Story, Ebba, 16, 218
superposed section, 46
Swede, George, 227n2

Tao, 113
Taylor, David, 37
Thoreau, Henry David, works of: "Autumnal Tints," xx; *Journal*, xiv, xv, xix; Kalendar project, 74, 90, 202; "Ktaadn," 7, 89; "A Natural History of Massachusetts," 89, 228n5; "Resistance to Civil Government," 144; "Walking," 14, 35, 125, 212, 213; *A Week on the Concord and Merrimack Rivers*, 15, 90
"Thoreau and the Haiku Spirit" (van den Heuvel), 14–15
Thurber, James, 207
Traces of Dreams (Shirane), 227n2
transcendentalism: kinship with Eastern philosophy, 15; kinship with haiku, 149; seeing nature as symbol of spirit, xv, 6, 47, 73, 198; Thoreau's practice of, 76, 89–90, 150, 224
Tripi, Vincent, 16
Trumbull, Charles, 227n2
Truth of Ecology, The (Phillips), 94

Updike, John, 137, 150

Van den Heuvel, Cor, 14–15

wabi: defined, xv, xxiv, 167; equated with simplicity, 95, 102, 109, 130, 195; indicated by humble and familiar things, 175, 225; related to Alec Therien, 131; related to Thoreau's life, 10–11, 89; related to Thoreau's prose, 99; related to Thoreau's sensibility, 102, 106
waka, xxv
Walden Pond, xvi, xx, 16, 152–53, 208, 215; compared to Bashō's "old pond," xiii–xiv, xix, 153, 155; conflated with *Walden* the book, 218; equated with the self, 151
"Walking" (Thoreau), 14, 35, 125, 212, 213
Washington, Peter, 15
Week on the Concord and Merrimack Rivers, A (Thoreau), 15, 90
Welch, Michael Dylan, 228n3
"When Lilacs Last in the Dooryard Bloom'd" (Whitman), 182
Whitman, Walt, 182
Wholeness and the Implicate Order (Bohm), 91–92
Williams, Terry Tempest, 37; *Refuge*, 94, 229–30n6
Williams, William Carlos, 123
"Winter Tracings and Transcendental Leaps" (Marshall), 187
wordlessness, xv, xxiv, 16, 50, 93

yōgen, xx, 47, 69, 73, 89, 95; in particular haiku, 149, 206, 223

zappai, xxi
Zen: associated with haiku, 13, 15, 26; Blyth's list of haiku's Zen attributes, 21, 30, 34, 56, 103; challenges to its association with haiku, 50, 201, 227–28n2; and physical labor, 136, 223
Zen Wave, A (Aitken), 227n2
zoku, 46–47